BEST WISHES

FOR A GREAT 2017

Clin

We create the world we describe

Listen to the Dolphins

by

Clive Bevan

Illustrated by Amy Ward

Work in progress

The challenge - do the right thing before the sun sets

This is a call to Leaders and Opinion Formers in organisations, schools and communities to address the issues of change, ahead of the time.

What legacy will you leave for those that follow you?

Will you be remembered as a Management, Union, Group, Team, School or Informal Leader or influencer who helped those around you address the issues of the future?

When will the sun set on your ability to influence the people who work with you and for what reason will your organisation remember you?

As the world changes around us, are your work teams setting new standards and staying ahead of the competition, or are you and your Colleagues working in the same old, same old way?

Are your work Colleagues; growing, learning, developing, adding more value than they did last month, through a structured action plan?

Is the talent in your organisation equal to the challenge?

Are you realising the potential in the people at all levels within your organisation?

Have you agreed your organisation's Purpose and aligned your Colleagues work effort with a Vision?

Can Colleagues describe their role in creating a competitive and more secure future?

If you find that you are not able to answer 'Yes' to most of these questions, then please recognise that its going to be dark soon. And that now is the time for you to help light up the way forward.

Learn the lessons of history and include some of the ideas in this book as you describe a new era.

Listen to the dolphins

This is a story about change set in the Firths around the Black Isle in Ross and Cromarty, Scotland. This part of the world has great; people, heritage, myths, truths, and was home to visionaries who told stories about future changes.

Imagine a unique solitude and peacefulness that only a long intriguing history can deliver. Add thousands of years of quiet Highland time, ancient battles, a few Clan feuds and then long, long, silences. Interrupted again by the noisy boys of war - when the North East of Scotland became home to eight air bases, and a refuge where the whole of the Naval fleet could anchor safely in the Cromarty Firth under well defended skies.

And when the wars ended and the planes migrated south, long silence returned until nuclear power was born in the far North when Harold Wilson announced that the 'white heat of technology - would fire Britain and the Cromarty Firth into a new, low- cost energy - era'.

The British Aluminium Company was to start an Aluminium smelter as a stable base loading for the new nuclear power stations. This would reduce the nation's balance of payments or at least the part that resulted from the import of three hundred thousand tonnes of aluminium, annually.

This venture was also the vehicle through which our nation planned to reverse the hundred year trends of people clearances from the Highlands. The area was to re-populate with priority jobs reserved for emigrants who wanted to return to their Highland home and heritage.

Homesteads were built and the small old settlements of Invergordon, Tain, Alness and Evanton were quickly overwhelmed with new houses and thousands of new people.

Even the Queen arrived to witness a house foundation mushroom into a fully fitted four bedroom detached during her eight hour visit. The area was subject to incredible change at close to reckless speed.

While the locals were adjusting to the fast pace of change, the incomers were adjusting to the opposite. The pubs closed at seven in the evening, as they had done since the war - to prevent the over lubrication of our armed forces - and there seemed to be no reason at all to change this forty year old tradition.

The hospital in Inverness was fifty miles away; a three hour round trip on a good traffic day. And Marks & Spencers was ten hours there and back with a guaranteed drop before you shop as well as during.

For old and new the pace of change in this part of the Highlands was incredible and then there was more. No sooner had the Smelter effect peaked when the North Sea oil industry kicked off and the whole area had another even bigger wave of growth and construction. Huge pipe line factories and oil rig fabricating yards sprung up and yet another surge of people swamped almost everything.

Now the founding fathers plans had said that the newcomers were to integrate with the local communities and this was an early success built on the daily work and social interaction of Highlanders and Lowlanders, they soon connected.

And the newcomers were also welcomed into the spirit of the Highlands through a dram, and a half, and a story, or a malt and sometimes all three and when the whisky flowed so did the spirit - through the folklore and the stories of the Highlands.

But there was a dark foreboding handed down through fireside story telling. An ancient sage called the Brahan Seer had predicted that there would be a great, silver, empty shed in the East and as with many of his tales, despair, and woe is us, was to befall the poor people in that area. Our real time story teller cautioned that many of his predictions had come true; we of course ignored this old message.

Despair, woe is us, and the enormous empty silver shed duly arrived just ten years later when between Christmas and New Year 1980 the smelter and a thousand employees were both victims of a - cyclical fall in aluminium prices - higher energy costs than expected - and the American part owners appetite to skulk back to the US with the money from the sale of its share. When the oil industry turned down too, this really was a desperate place.

Boom to bust in fifteen years, high hopes one day, lowest despair the next, riches to rags, and all of this witnessed by a school of dolphins who followed the tide in and out of the Firth every single day throughout all of time.

The school had squeaked at Winston Churchill on the Alness river bank, led our Naval fleet out to war in 1940. Chaperoned the forty thousand ton alumina cargo on the SS Richard to its first berth on the smelter jetty in 1971 and helped push the first North Sea oil platform out of Nigg bay into the deep sea.

They had indeed seen it all and add to this their outstanding ability to hand down stories accurately from Elders to Youngers over thousands of years - leaves us thinking that we can learn a great deal - if we listen to and understand the lessons from the world as described by a Dolphin.

As you read the story we hope that ideas and questions will pop in your head.

Have a stock of post its ready - log your thoughts, one per post it - and attach to the notes pages left blank for this purpose.

We create the world that we describe

Jess lived in a cottage right next to the Cromarty Firth and loved to swim near to where the dolphins played on most days in her school holidays.

They often swam quite close to her but none of the many close encounters had prepared her for the day that Flipper – one of the pod leaders – almost stood up in front of her and said ' hello I'm Flipper and I know that your name is Jess'. He continued - 'You're a bright young girl; now tell me, have you heard the story of Pliny the Younger'?

'No sir', said Jess 'I haven't'.

'You haven't? He was born in the 30's; you must have heard of him, his famous Uncle died trying to help people just after the volcano erupted'.

'Would that be Mount St Helens' said Jess knowingly?

'Oh no my dear it was Mt. Vesuvius in the August of 79, seventy nine years after Jesus died. You see Pliny was a Roman Leader, an aristocrat, an author, a writer of detailed letters; on Empire, Government, culture, organisations, and of course dolphins. He told the story of a tame dolphin - some of us say - this tells us a great deal about you humans.

The story was first written by his Uncle. And we think that he must have forgotten that this wasn't his story. Others say that this doesn't really matter - as long as we learn from the tale anyway.

We dolphins always make a point of telling our youngsters all the stories we know, so that we can help them learn from our experience, and most of all we want to help them base their decisions on facts.

7

Let's start off with a fishy fact and for this I'll need to ask you a question.

What is the most dangerous and big, big, biggest animal family in the sea?'

Jess thought, 'that… that would be a shark' and she gave - 'shark family' - as her final answer. 'No, no my dear' said the dolphin; 'there is a much bigger killer in the sea'.

Now killer was the key word and instantly Jess said 'a killer whale'.

'You are very close' said the dolphin, 'now my question was; what is the most dangerous, big, big, animal *family* in the sea? '

'A killer whale family' said Jess.

'No, no, no', said the dolphin as he spluttered and tried to contain his smirks and giggles. 'It's us, it's us', he said as he clapped his fins and bounced up and down, 'genus Orcinus or Orca to his friends, is as dolphin as I am, my posh name is genus Tursiops and we all belong to the same Dolphin family.

You see, this is where the facts in life, are not always easy to find. When you watch dolphins surfing the waves, leaping out of the water, chasing fish, outpacing the front of a high speed boat - or just playing around in the water - you would never guess that Orca the bloodful - seal eater extraordinaire - was one of us.' he said.

'And now back to Pliny the Younger who pinched the story from Pliny the Elder, well the Elder didn't have the facts either - but at least he was recording what was true to him at the time. You see Pliny wrote the story of the tame dolphin, who came to the bay to play, and swam near the fishing boats and even jumped for the small fish that the fisherman threw.

This was one of the earliest texts recording man connecting with dolphins and the start of human descriptions of us - 'as perhaps the most intelligent animals on Earth' - and all of this because we tell our youngsters to keep a very keen eye and stay real close, to anything that moves in the whole of the ocean.

You see Jess, what Pliny didn't realise was that dolphins just naturally work best in teams - called Pods - of between ten and twenty, and we network together to seek out and harvest fish.

And when we find a really big shoal, we text our mates and can congregate in hundreds and even thousands - the bigger the shoal of fish, the more dolphins we invite and everyone gets to eat really well.'

'But we can't really fish on our own, so when you see one dolphin, in a bay, he's probably lost - and when he's feeding from the fisherman he's really hungry.

It's usually the older, aggressive males, who think they know it all, and who might have been encouraged to leave the Pod that end up on their lonesome.

The fact is that whilst Pliny believed that this was a tame dolphin who liked people - we know that he was just an ageing old flipper with out of date skills, battling against an out going tide and running out of time.

This is why we hand down our stories from generation to generation, so that our youngsters can better understand what really is and what really isn't.

Just like you Jess' he continued, 'lots of humans could be describing the dolphin who prefers people to flippers - but now you have some facts - and you can tell a different story.

But be careful, you might have the facts, but others may not be ready or even want to hear them. We'll talk about humans and dolphins and the games we play later and I will explain how the Pod works best for all of us.

My Granddad told me about Pliny the Elder, and everyone in our Pod knows the real story. And when you grow up, you can tell all of your little sprogs and they can tell their children, and over time all of your family will be better informed and wiser.

Well Jess, the world was not as Pliny described it.

If you replay the scene today, form a similar picture in your head - the Romans net fishing from a boat – in an Italian bay.

This time add in; the dolphin was ageing - had lost his buddies - because he hadn't behaved well, couldn't catch fish on his own, and was more than happy to let the fishermen feed him.

Now you understand the real story.

What has Jess learned today?

Man and dolphins have talked about each other for ever. But the dolphin's view of the world is different from mans.

The Plinys were world experts at recording and communicating and describing Roman times. Their writings are studied by scholars to this day.

On Dolphin Bay, they described what they saw – truthfully - they recorded what was true to them. Soon many reading Romans believed the same story.

Meanwhile, all of us, the dolphins that is - described something different. We believe our story, this is our truth.

Now the Romans were big on Pods too, they formed small groups and senates and Legions, and then they conquered the world.

Funny really, from these ancient times, Romans were advanced enough to conquer the world that they described. However, even their most learned scholars were describing the wrong things about dolphins

And until we talked today, no one had combined these beliefs into one. It's good to talk – and of great value when you know how to listen.

Jess wanted to listen again tomorrow, what new stories and understandings would she build then?

'What had the old dolphin done that was so bad? I wouldn't like to do that to my Granddad' she thought.

Well, what do you know?

Jess woke early and went outside the small house on the Moray Firth. This was an excellent place to meet and chat with her very own Flipper. Jess could see the Pod a few hundred metres away and she wiggled her feet in the water until Flipper arrived.

Flipper's opening question was always, 'Well, what do you know?'

'Not very much' said Jess 'but I learned a lot yesterday. I e-mailed my Granddad and told him our story and said that he wasn't to worry. And I promised him that when he became old and grumpy that we wouldn't send him off to an old people's home.

What do your young dolphin's think when their Granddad disappears?'

'Well Jess, it is a last resort and I need to tell you more about how we survive by working together and I'll start with a question - this one is a two part question, but not a multiple choice'.

'Have you seen dolphins outpace and swim faster than a boat'?

'Yes' said Jess, 'we watch the dolphins swim ahead of even very fast boats'

'Are we the fastest thing that lives in the sea around here?' asked Flipper. 'Yes' said Jess.

No, no, no we are not' laughed Flipper, 'it's the fish who are the fastest. Well, I suppose you are right and you are wrong', said Flipper. 'Fact is that we are definitely faster than anything of our size or bigger, and much much faster than a human in the water.

We need to be to be able to catch the very, very, fast fish - they are the fastest things in the sea round here - those mackerel can really motor'.

Jess looked on engrossed as he continued 'As we surf along the beach in a Pod, one of us will see a fish, and then we need to move as quickly as we can. Whoever sees the fish becomes our leader.

'Fish supper at eight o'clock' says Dorcas, and someone immediately heads towards six o'clock and someone to ten o'clock. Dorcas heads straight for the fish, and we all maintain radio silence. The rest of the Pod swims to all of the other points on the clock so that the fish is surrounded. As the whole Pod moves, other fish may surface but where ever they swim we have the whole area covered'.

Wilma actually caught the fish and thanked Dorcas. The whole Pod swam close to her and gave her a thank you nudge. 'Us dolphins don't say too much to each other - we communicate more through behaviour than words - swim close to each other - like sardines in a sandwich' said Flipper.

'Pliny the Roman was right about one thing, we may well be the most intelligent animal family on the earth. But some of us say you humans could catch us up, eventually, and especially if you understand how a dolphin team works.'

Flipper explained this in more detail. 'First and foremost we understand that the most effective leadership of a team is shared leadership. And we are all ready to lead on our little patch, when opportunity creates a need.

As we patrol the beach and surf the waves, everyone chatters, you can hardly get a high pitched squeak in edgeways, it's like chaos café. We don't call this communicating, this is just aimless chatter. When Dorcas says 'fish at six o'clock' we only have one voice, Dorcas leads, we listen, 'fish moving to seven thirty'; we respond silently, one fish, one voice, is the golden rule.

But we don't stay dumb for long. Dimus says 'fish two at nine o'clock' and part of the Pod breaks off to cover Dimus at eight o'clock and ten o'clock, and when we hit a shoal we could have eight leaders heading off in different directions, with Pod followers responding to the lead.'

'What is really important is that everyone understands the base rules and this is where Dorcas has a powerful influence'.

Chances are Dorcas will not catch the first fish, someone at seven o'clock or even eight o'clock will catch fish number one.

As soon as Dorcas hears Dimus break radio silence and say fish two at eight o'clock our rules say the leader stops fishing. Swims to the surface - jumps right out of the water and decides how big the shoal really is.

She then communicates. Big shoal heading west, and immediately texts our buddy Pods. We can have fifty or sixty dolphins homing in with just one clear directional message from Dorcas.

Dorcas understands the big picture and whilst the rest of us focus on the task, she manages the overall coordination process. For example, if we are heading north, and the fish turn right, we're heading straight into the main shipping lane.'

'This could cause bad news headlines' said Jess -'dolphin head butts boat- Uh Oh'.

Flipper continued, 'Dorcas organises Pods two and three to help us turn the fish to the left, into the Cromarty Firth.

Here our biggest risk is a slow moving oil rig - trundling - at half the speed of a barnacle after a night out on the seaweed juice. In these waters it's just us and the fish, no danger, and we can get the job done.

Fish are very tricky you know, and this job isn't easy. Just ask the Fortrose fishermen, they can be out on the sea for a week and come back with a bucketful of prawns and not much else.

Pod communications need to be excellent and our actions efficient. Our first rule - be ready to focus on the job in hand - when the fish arrive we move into overdrive.

There are five or six experienced leaders in our Pod of twenty - they can all lead really well. We know who they are. Any one can lead on fish one, but as soon as someone breaks the fish one silence by saying fish two, one of our established leaders takes over.

Team one, on fish one, proceed on their own, team two on fish two proceed on their own, but the twenty Pod is now led by Dorcas whose job it is to coordinate the bigger picture. And we self organise, leading or following as needed to do the job.'

'Dorcas has an important role within the team,' said Jess, how does she manage to keep everyone tuned in to what is going on?

Whoever Leads has our full support, we discuss the rights and wrongs later.

The best Leaders always listen to those around them.

Everyone understands Pod systems and structures.

Within this frame work the team makes Dorcas's difficult job easier.

Post its or notes pages

Our Team's intelligence system is different

'Our youngsters understand that there are three parts to Dolphin speak - you call it Communication. The first is Chatter, random noise from everyone to everyone. Have a nice day exchanges; thank you for that, good morning, well hello, and what is your news? These are good examples of the Chattering class messages.

We differentiate Chatter from Communication, by describing *Communication, as things we might need to know.*

For example, we tune in at ten to six every night to Radio Four, and really listen when a man says, ' Sea areas; Hebrides, North Sea, Cromarty - wind force six building to gale force eight by 04.00 hrs'.

Who knows where we'll be by 04.00 tomorrow? The weather forecast is part of a wide range of intelligence that we might need to help us catch fish, safely. If the shoals take us towards the North Sea in the early hours, we know that we need to fish from the top down and under the big rolling waves.

Other Pods Communicate regularly by text: 'Good day yesterday, just off Inverness harbour'. Caught eighty seven fish with a fourteen dolphin Pod in three hours. With a catch performance of eighty OFR - overall fish rate.

We also communicate general facts that we and others might need to know.

On this weekend last year the weather was warm and the mackerel came in. Ten Pods of twenty dolphins with an overall fish success rate of ninety two - just South of the Orkney Islands - it was manic. Mackerel mania has to be seen to be believed.

There is a whole range of knowledge in the - might need to know category- that could be useful to other pods and leaders - we call this Communication.'

Jess was sponging up all the information as Flipper delivered and she lent closer towards the water to be sure not to miss a word.

He continued, 'Now I have to say that none of the *Chatter or even Communication* is considered to be the most important part of dolphin-speak. The most important part of all is *Information*.

Information is a high level intelligence that everyone needs to know - rules*, behaviours, and word messages that help us clear confusion.* This is really useful when we are under pressure.

Can you imagine the turmoil when everyone is working at full throttle, in the middle of a high speed chase?

Fish swarm in every direction but which way; right, left, up, down, slow left, fast dive right. If we all described where they were going we really would end up in ever decreasing whirl pools.

We rely on every dolphin to work to our base rules - keep the shoal moving left - swallow any fish on your left - but don't stop - keep them moving. And even though you might be really busy, with your mouth full of fish, keep your ears open for a message from Dorcas. 'Pod two coming in from seven o'clock to turn the shoal left'. Everyone knows what to do to move the shoal in the right direction.

And some times even more important *Information* clicks in - Dorcas to Pod - '*Shark coming in – left of the sun beams - circle right, until it swallows three fish, and then drifts off'*.

Dorcas knows that the shark always dives straight in, and always swerves left - 'move to ten o'clock now,' no one argues, everyone obeys the message.

Information – is the intelligence that we need to help us do a good job and stay safe.

This is the knowledge that helps us clear confusion. Whenever we are unsure about what to do, we do what Dorcas does, or ask someone.

We have learned not to stay in one area - swimming in circles on our ownsome - worrying about the shark - this is not a good idea.

You see Jess, the most important rules that help us live, play, eat and stay safe are included in the *Information pack* that all new Pod members receive. We learn the general rules and then we work to them, our sea can be a really dangerous place.

And on this very point - the rules that is - the problems started with Grumpus. That was the real name of the dolphin in Pliny's bay - all those years ago. But before we discuss what didn't work too well lets review what does work well. I need to rejoin the Pod and fish for a while.

We'll meet again in the morning, and you can tell me what you remember from today.

E mail your Granddad, he's probably still worried, and he might be able to explain more about your slow motion - communication in teams - compared to our Ocean wide mega byte broad band system.

'OK will do' said Jess as a voice in her head said 'hmmm - I'll need to simplify this a bit before talking to Granddad.'

These pages are for your notes

Granddad, why can't I sleep when I'm thinking about stuff?

This wasn't the question that Jess had planned to ask. It was however the first one to pop into her mind.

Granddad said, 'no need to worry, I do it, all the time darling, just ask your head to simplify the question. Then give your head an answer, then zzz….zzzz until morning time.

There will be times when the mind monster climbs out of its cage and just continues to talk to you, when you just want to go to sleep.

What was the little talking computer that you had - was it called - an Omygotchi ? It used to say; 'feed me, smooth me, please change my diaper and I love you.

Well a mind monster is a similar beastie - quite demanding - needing attention, but this time the computer is a nice little voice inside your head.'

Fact is that when your head has issues it keeps coming up with answers, even when you are asleep. And sometimes wakes you up to tell you all about the new solutions or just to ask you more questions.

The next time the monster wakes you up, call up a nice picture in your mind - try the sledging in the snow on a sunny morning - picture. Then, at the same time, quietly- slooow the voice in your head wooords down, breathe deeply, look up into your eyelids and relax. You'll soon move back into sleep time.

Granddad, I've been talking to our dolphin, about messaging and he suggested I talk to you.'

Granddad smiled quietly at the speed at which Jess had changed the subject of the discussion. Quicker than an eye blink and she was off on to the next topic. Need to keep up he thought.

Jess continued with high speed chat. 'Flipper said that you might know the human form of their Dolphin speak the equivalent of our Communication - it has three parts; Chatteration, Communication, and Information'

'Ah this I do understand', says Granddad. 'Chatteration is what makes the world go around, and helps messages move from one person to another. It starts somewhere and can end up anywhere and everywhere.

This is the way that humans acknowledge each other and just pass the time of day, these words don't usually mean very much. It's the words equivalent of giving your seat up to an old lady on the bus; it is a nice and considerate thing to do.

Communication is what people might need to know and it's more important than Chatteration. This is how one part of the village gets to know what the other people are doing and how one work team gets to know what another work team is up to.

These messages can go a very long way - we had a fault on our new telephone and the man who fixed it messaged all of the other men in his team - and said 'the Gloucester new spot phone is a pig of a thing to repair.

Try straightening the antennae at the back of phone first, this one was curly and straightening it worked today'. Everyone texted back and said 'Thanks Buddy.'

Then there was the lorry driver, who saw a big pile of kitchen tissues ready for delivery to Inverness store, but he was there only yesterday and you couldn't move in the store room for tissues.

He called the store and right enough the computer was wrong. If he hadn't Communicated the store would have had more of what it didn't need and there would have been even less room for the deliveries that they did need.

Local Information is probably the most important of all. Every team needs to know what to do when they have a problem and especially what to do when they think something isn't right.

A clearly visible, local plan, explaining who does what by when, is the most important factor in delivering results.

And yes each team needs to know where they are against the plan, where they fit in the bigger plan, and be able to track their own progress.

'Jess, it's time that you went to sleep. We can talk again tomorrow. Night God bless darling.'

Whilst Jess slept, Granddad e mailed her the update;

Dolphins understand Communication better than we do

There is a system and structure to life and work in the Pod

Pod members understand the rules

Everyone Chatters but right place- right time

When the work starts the Pod self organises

No one needs to give orders

Early on in the chase anyone can lead and everyone else will follow

When there are just two or three tasks Plan A works

Someone Communicates when the Pod needs to work differently

As work complicates they all know who will manage the bigger picture. This work is different, new skills needed from the leader and a broader range of rules in the team

In work time - we have a one voice discipline

Everyone listens to understand - example - we are escalating to Plan B

Small teams, self organise locally, within the bigger organisational network

Multi task- team work, needs clear overall direction

Most all everyone has had an input to Plan A, B and C -
before these plans are needed

The most important Pod skill is **listening**

Intuitive, structured, systematic, responsive,dynamic, responsible, are all key words in the Dolphin work systems.

*- **Work team systems understood by all.***

*- **Structured effective team process.***

*- **Self organising.***

*- **Leaders coordinate the bigger picture***

Chatter

Communication

Information

What we need to know
to deliver the Plan Safely

It's a new day and Jess learns how to listen

Jess opened her e - mail before she had opened her eyes properly. Everyone else in the family was in bed and the start up music on the computer didn't wake anyone, so she read Granddad's mail in the hushed, silent house.

'My Granddad really does know a lot' thought Jess 'even though he is old, very, very old. I wonder if he knew a Roman, must ask him'.

The sea was flat calm and in the distance Jess heard a bump thud, bump thud noise and eventually a fishing boat rounded the headland and sailed home towards Inverness harbour.

Enter stage left, the dolphin Pod welcoming party, they swam at the front of the boat, chattering and surfing on the bow waves. 'Nothing like an early morning blast to clear the underwater spider's cob webs' said one to the other.

After a while a few dropped off the chase and then they all turned and headed back towards Cromarty. The fishing boat was rather slow, they had tried to encourage it to go faster, but it could only work at bump and thud, bump and thud - speed.

'How on earth, or in the water, could they catch any fish at all', thought Hamish, he was Pod member number eighteen, a bright young two year old.

He thought it over and then decided that perhaps they catch the fish when they turn the other way and swim towards the nets. Hmm must ask someone.

But what Hamish was really clear about were the rules about fishing boats; bump thud, bump thud means a boat is coming. When the Chatter starts we track the direction and then follow the sound.

And remember, that there is always bad news at the back of the boat - so we recite to ourselves - bump thud, stay at the front, bump thud, stay at the front. A simple message that keeps all dolphins out of harms way.

As the Pod slivered slowly back, Flipper told everyone he was going to chat to Jess who had walked down to the jetty, and that he would catch them up soon. Jess was splashing her feet in the cold water.

'Well, what do you know?' says Flipper.

Quick as a flash Jess says, 'Well I think it is my turn to ask you a starter for ten question, and the subject for this round is Granddads, you have two minutes and you'll need to answer quickly.

Last night, right, the whole house was Chattering.

The television was on, Grandma was talking to Mum, my little sister was playing her noisy Nintendo and I was thinking about what you said about everyone in the Pod listening to each other.

Then I remembered that Granddad's e-mail had said that listening is the most important part of communication. So my question is 'how do you know when you are listening?'

'Jess, that is a great question!' Flipper jumped out of the water and clapped his flippers, 'because you have asked the right question first, I know that you have been listening, to me and to your Granddad!' Jess smiled.

'The most important part of the process that you call Communication is **Listening**, and we tell every young dolphin that when they are listening, they will be working hard at understanding what the other person is saying, and, and, and,' he was getting

30

really excited, '*and - **you will not be thinking about what you are going to say next.***

You see Jess in our Pod we have to think ten times faster than the fish and this is five times faster than you humans. We watch your lot swimming in the water, and we understand why you use the term - too slow to catch a cold. You are so slow that you definitely won't be catching a fish.

Humans can talk at 250 words per minute, and you can think at 450 words per minute. We dolphins talk at 1250 words per minute - except Dorcas who is from Dublin and she can reach 1300, when excited – and we think at over 2000 words per minute.

Fast movers need to be even faster thinkers.

Problem is that when we think at this speed, the think box - the body part between our ears - is whizzing information around like elvers in a fast flowing current. Everyone thinking twice as fast as they can talk- and listening becomes difficult.

"Jess, you will be listening when you are not thinking about anything else."

And of greatest importance, you will not be thinking about what you are going to say next'. This is so easy to say but it takes lots of practice to be able to listen. You really need to tune in to what others are saying to you.

When we do fishing work with a shoal on our patch, Chattering stops immediately. As soon as someone says 'haddock on toast at five o'clock', everyone moves into action and listens in, so that we all know what to do next.

Communication lines are always open, Hamish says 'haddock at five o'clock'- Marcia says, 'haddock at nine o'clock - Dorcas peels off to the right, scans the bigger picture and then tells everyone how big the opportunity is and decides if we need another Pod's help.

Information, the knowledge flow that helps us do a good job safely - shoal moving towards shipping lane, bump thud, bump thud approaching fast at four hundred meters - is a really important thing to know, and all of this depends on listening'.

As they talked the sea was flat and calm, the tide was in and the waves were splashless. Silence was everywhere, and there was a lot of listening going on.

Jess teased Flipper, 'You'll need to speed up your answers, if you want to score points' said Jess. 'And the first question on Granddad's across the ages is - why was Pliny's dolphin excluded from the Pod?'

'I don't think I'm going to score many points here Jess as you keep asking the right questions, the problem is there are no short answers'.

'OK' said Jess, 'I'll stop asking difficult questions and you can tell me the long answer stories.'

'Well' said Flipper 'Grumpus wasn't fitting in with the Pod, he was complicating life for everyone. Sometimes he would be talking to himself, loudly, even when we were right next to a big shoal.

We were unable to get near the fish, they always heard his booming voice first and even in Chatter time you heard his voice longest and loudest.

Things took a turn for the worst when Sharon's youngest became so weak, for the lack of food, that the whole Pod had to slow down. We were eating less and less every day.

Eventually three of us stayed behind with Sharon, and Grumpus. And the rest went off to find fish, before we all starved.

They were back in just two hours with fish for everyone and indigestion for Sharon - she just wouldn't chew her food properly - but Grumpus centred hunger was a lesson that we had to learn from.

Grumpus was really important to us, he had taught us much of what we knew, but times had changed, and much of his knowledge was based on what used to work.

Months went by before he really listened to us on the frightening the fish front, and years passed as we tried to persuaded him that the story from Pliny's bay wasn't really useful anymore.

The world had changed, he was still working on splash, splash, splash – silence - and look out for the small net that the Romans used to fish with. The rest of us had moved on to bump-thud many years since.

And he really did think that the Russian mother ship, anchored off Oban, was an island, and he caused mayhem and panic by describing the submarine that always works in that area as the biggest shark he had ever seen.

What are the words that dolphins recite to remind them of dangers at the back end of the boat?

---- ---- swim -- --- -----

Simple messages are best.

Better not confuse Chatter with Information

Grumpus had described what he remembered from his frightening and confusing close encounter with something really big and grey, in the sea, off Oban.

'It had an enormous mouth, green eyes and black teeth'. This was what he described, in vivid detail, to everyone - as he Chattered at the play group.

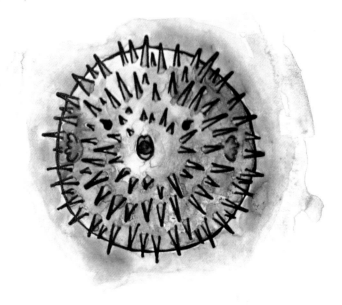

The youngsters didn't sleep for a week. As the story circulated the Pod the shadowy beast just got bigger and bigger. Mothers were frantic, and two of the children had to take cod liver oil pills for a month as they were disrupting the classroom.

'What will Grumpus say next?' Was the in-question at the Chattering classes. Problem was everyone started to believe the message, it was like a seaweed vine, it grew and it grew.

I think you might call it a grape vine. It's where a message is passed around like - Alice kissed Jamie in the play ground. But the story teller leaves out - after he had fallen over - and that she was only applying the Granddad solution to every fall - let me kiss it better. Suddenly the seaweed vine message said that he was her boy friend. This just wasn't true but that didn't stop the chatter.

Sea weed vines are really powerful. In Ireland and the Scottish Islands they put out of date sea weed on potatoes, and they grow bigger, how powerful is that?'

And so it was with the shark tale. Its teeth got bigger the tail longer and it became more and more frightening every time the story was told. Grumpus added more gory detail every time he told the story until the whole Pod shivered at the thought.

Asking Grumpus to leave was the last thing that anyone in the Pod really wanted to do. But this wasn't the first time he had caused chaos.

Pod leaders decided that he should attend a Communications and Diversity course at the University of Atlantis.

He was analysed by a PhD Sea horse, who told him he had to describe a new world and that by describing it he would start to make progress towards it.

According to - "new Grumpus," as he now called himself - Chattering was an important part of our lives. We should say hello to every barnacle we met, even the crusty old ones, everyone needs to be noticed and acknowledged.

And we should all question Chatterboxes. It was helpful and OK to challenge the grapevine and really important to do so before everyone starts to believe the wrong messages.

36

His course had considered a number of real examples where the grapevine had impacted on a whole Community.

Grumpus off Oban, proved to be the best case study. The students decided that Grumpus's nightmare story could have changed if someone had asked the right questions.

 When Grumpus had said, he had seen a one hundred meter long, grey shark with green eyes. If anyone had asked him, 'are you sure it was a shark?'

He might have said yes, but at the very least he would have asked himself the question again. And if they still weren't sure, they could have asked more questions.

'Did the shark have an engine?'

'Well er um, now that you ask, it did have a very quiet bump-thud. Yes, I think it did' said Grumpus.

'If you saw a shark this big, you wouldn't have hung around to check it's dental records would you?

Were you frightened and confused as to what to do next- other than applying Pod law number one- see shark - retreat stage right and rapid'?

'Yes I was both frightened and confused even my flippers were flustered,' said Grumpus.

'Do you now think it might have been something else?'

 Grumpus didn't need to answer.

If the right questions had been asked at the right time.

The story would have been different.

And then perhaps, just maybe, Grumpus wouldn't have given the children nightmares'.

Only the brave question the Grapevine

Flipper listened as Grumpus continued his University of Atlantis saga.

'On the training course one delegate had told the class that un-questioned Chatter and grapevine had led to allegations of bullying at his workplace.

The story passed from desk to desk and soon everyone was saying that the Manager was bullying them too. When in fact she was really only doing her job.

It took one person to be big enough to say that she was not bullying. As a matter of fact she was doing what was right - then the chatter message changed.

Another delegate told the story that the grapevine grew racist branches too. A few words taken out of context led to - 'he is a racist because he said Tumble weed'.

Now everyone knew that you are not allowed to have Tumble weed on your packaging. It is the generic name for all underwater weeds, but the Sea weeds find the term offensive.

This grape vine grew branch after branch, someone else said 'he called me a Weedie wimp' and before anyone realised the Chatter turned into a Racist rant.

Fortunately one brave scallop said, 'why don't you clam up - I will say that this guy is not a Racist - and I think we need to differentiate between the unfortunate and innocent words that he used, and what he really stands for.

I can think of a number of occasions where he has intervened in a way that communicates racial equity as opposed to discrimination'. The Chatter stopped when facts intervened. Some didn't like it, but at least - *folk could now be proud of what they were Chattering about.'*

McTavish - another student - told the course delegates that when the kitchen burned down in Fort William that all of the following reasons came up on the grapevine; arson, insurance claim, vendetta from a sacked employee, and the Wee Free Presbyterians claiming it was an act of God.

They had all been accepted as true reasons for the event until the assistant Chef told the real story about a cooking chips hiccup after a night on the bevy.

Corporal McPhee - another delegate - said that he had heard that Saddam Hussein had dismantled all of his weapons of mass destruction before we invaded Iraq. And that the only weapon he had left was his sabre, to rattle at George Bush.

Meanwhile, Tony Blair was telling us that the enemy were one hour's flight time away from bombing London. McPhee wondered if it was a nuclear sabre, or just an echo of something that George Bush's Dad had told him about cowboys in Iraq, or was it Iran?

Grumpus told us that we should all question the grapevine and search out the facts.

And yes whilst bullying, racism, arson and why did we go to war, are issues of a much higher order - him telling the playgroup about a mega shark turned out not to be true either - he had thought it was - but it wasn't.'

The University had started a Grapevine challenge, and had used Grumpus as the example. If someone had asked him, *do you think* it was a shark, or *do you know*?' He would have said that 'he thought it was' and in the telling realised that he needed more facts - before it became a story that he was proud to pass on to others.

And most of all Grumpus had learned from his mistake and now knew that Chattering without facts could do great harm and even cost someone their reputation - and others their lives.

'So Jess, when someone says - she is not nice, or - he is not friendly, always expect the best from people, and ask the person who is peddling the message for more facts.

Don't be afraid to say – 'every one of us can be friendly and when people get worked up, and angry, we need to understand why'.

Most bullies are frightened of something, and most of all they need help. Understanding, based on facts always helps.

'I need some facts', said Jess. You still haven't told me why Grumpus needed to go'.

'That's right' said Flipper 'but before I do will you summarise what you, Granddad and I have said about Communication and Dolphin speak?

'Must dash, I have just two hours to prepare for a talk to the Women's Institute. Heavens to albatross, they want to do a mermaid calendar for next year called Wrinklies on the Rocks - this is not a good idea,' said Flipper shuddering.

'Wrinklies on the rocks - that sounds like a good theme for a whisky advert - said Jess, 'The W.I. squad like a nippie sweetie. Persuade them that wee dram stories down the ages might be a better topic.'

Jess summarised as follows:

Listening is the most important part of communicating

You listen best, when you are not thinking of what you will say next

Enjoy Chattering with everyone you meet

Expect the best from everyone, you might get it

Effective communication in a team needs one voice, everyone else listens, to understand

Simple messages are best – bump thud, bump thud, swim at the front

Search out the facts. Is it fact or is it fiction?

Do you think its true - do you know it is true?

We need to be proud of what we Chatter about.

Question the facts in the grapevine before you join the messengers. Stand up and speak your mind, when the grapevine may be off message.

Chatter can be both mindless and dangerous in unfair circumstances.

From school bully groups, through small people networks, bad guys and girls seek to increase their power and influence through chatter-mongering.

It takes a brave person to be the one in the group that says 'is that true'?

Or to say 'you are not being fair on the poorly dressed girl'.

Many of today's work bullies would have been described as firm and fair in the past – but when the bully message grapevine starts its voice can grow.

Political game players use the Racist card and this can spread like a virus when others join in.

These games stop when you require the truth, the facts, the evidence.

When McT's kitchen burned down there were five versions of the truth.

When America invaded Cuba in 1961 and Iraq in March 2003 neither the decision makers, nor the populations at large were given the facts.

In 2006 two soldiers were dying every day in Iraq, seven hundred of our armed forces per year and countless thousands of Iraq's fighters and civilians.

Are we still repeating the errors of past eras?

Flipper had said 'I don't think you humans have learned too much in forty man years'

Organisations need systems and structures to sniff out the facts. Before the; claim, counter claim, she said, he said, we are all saying- escalator- takes far too many issues to the top of the organisation.

Completely unfounded bully, racist, sexist and general unfairness claims can take years to kill off when the grapevine has taken root.

Our schools, clubs, and organisations need mechanisms to engage the people who drive the critical stories up the spiral - in the design of the solutions.

*The **organisations values** need to become a foundation block as you build great places to work and to learn in.*

We will not tolerate poor behaviour .

This includes unfounded rumour.

Is that story fact or fiction ?

Do you think or do you know ?

Are you proud of what you chatter about ?

The dynamics of the dolphin Pod

'Flipper, my Granddad really needs to know why Grumpus had to go', said Jess, taking the questioning initiative again. 'And by the way did you manage to talk April out of her swim suit at the Women's Institute?'

'Piece of fish cake' said Flipper 'they were like porpoise putty in my paws. My talk on - wee dram adverts across the ages - and the free samples from the Teaninich distillery - went down a treat. Thanks for that.

You see Jess, getting it right as a Pod of dolphins means we survive, getting it wrong means we die.

The way we are and the way we work has been fashioned through years and years of analysing what works, and learning from what doesn't.

We have an age old understanding that our Pods work well with fifteen to twenty dolphins and we can build this number over a few years, mainly as a result of twitter pattering.

We do a lot of twitter pattering. Some say we think of little else and baby dolphins arrive all the time.

And we really do need to be careful about who we twitter patter with because many, many years ago everyone almost became related to everyone else.

Dorcas was someone's sister and they were related to the dolphins around the corner, and Hamish was having a fling with his second cousin. You didn't know what to say to whom, in case they were related.

We had just decided that we needed to introduce some new blood when everything went awfully wrong and Orca went off the rails.

Orca was a weight lifter and we think he over dosed on steroids. He became so big that small fish couldn't satisfy him. As he got bigger and bigger, he ate more and more salmon. Trouble was they had escaped from a fish farm and had been fed on man made proteins.

Well, the combination of steroids and fish farm food meant that he developed white patches of skin and huge teeth. Fortunately for him Anna went anabolic as well and they went off and started their own Orca family.

Every seal in the wide world regrets the day and we don't talk about them, as one of us, any more - we are fisher folk - they are butchers.

However, there was a constructive outcome from this event. It made us think, and we decided that if we failed to control our gene bank we might turn into Orcas as well.

Two messages went out to everyone, the first; you are not to kiss your cousins, and the second, please encourage suitable dolphins from other Pods to join yours.

As a result our Pods became bigger, quicker, and we realised through experience that when we grew to more than twenty - the best thing to do was to start a new Pod.

We also found that when we hit a big shoal, inviting thirty dolphins in - only worked well if they were two Pods of about fifteen - who had a similar work system, ethics and values - as we did. Any old dolphins wouldn't do, so Dorcas knows who to call when we need help.

And knowing what to do was something that didn't figure in Pod - think when Marvin came on the scene.

Marvin arrived on the off chance just as we needed help with a mackerel moment and partnered very well with Marcia - too well some say.

They had a ball and we all ate and drank far too much to notice that Marvin was mooching in on Marcia delivering flipper fulls of mussels off the legs of an oil rig.

We had been a settled Pod for ages, working together, playing together and had grown to eighteen strong over a five year period. Within the Pod we had a good balance of leaders and followers.

Steady Eddie, jolly Jane, Buster the thruster, and a few hard nuts like Hazel all moulded over time into a powerbase. No one argued with Hazel, she was a powerful and wise woman, had a vicious tail on her when in a flap.

Hazel had four buddies that she spent a lot of time with, and Buster had his followers too. In both of these camps they seemed to have a similar view of the sea bed - one group said one thing and the other group usually suggested something different but having squabbled over what was right and what was wrong for so many years, no one became heated in the arguments.

Until the day that Marvin argued with Hazel about the best place to find cockles and Marcia took Marvin's side.'

'Well, sea war four hundred and eighty three broke out. Hazel screamed, 'what does he know, he's only been here five minutes. I've been here for thirty years and I have seen guys like him come and go. And as for you Marcia, you are just a tart! I remember when you buddied up with that oyster for four days, just because he promised you a pearl!'

There is no fury on the bottom of the sea like Hazel scorned, she went from one episode of history to the next until Marcia was in tears.

Jane went to comfort her and then Hazel opened up with both flippers. 'And as for you Jane - you shouldn't say one word, or I will tell everyone about you dancing on the table, singing love on the rocks at the Christmas party. You know what trouble that got you into!'

'Fact is Jess, that the closer the bond in the team, the longer that people have worked together, the more fixed everyone becomes in their ways. And when anyone tries to introduce a change, or introduce someone new, there is often so much group anger and heat that you can cook mussels in the water.

Hazel had always led us to the best cockle beds. She said turn left, and we did, and it worked, year after year she was the main cockle day Co-ordinator.

Tis true we hadn't done very well in the previous weeks and a few of us were wondering - has she lost it? We had held a quick ballot by chatter and the majority were still with her. Then, when Marvin said 'why don't we turn right' - our doubts balloon went up again, turmoil followed.

Hazel's mob just swam into a circle around her, and Buster's gang went to support Marvin.

Everyone swam around in circles nattering and chattering at each other until Hazel's group decided that her idea to swim to the left was right and Buster's group decided that right was right.

The Pod fractured into two separate groups. Each group nuzzled the sand and gathered the cockles, but unfortunately Hazel had hit another bad patch. We think that Marvin knew that the migrant cockle fishers had cleaned that bed out - but Hazel didn't.

Jane, Eddie and Hamish started to swim in a wider circle and they slowly and unknowingly drifted away from Hazel. As they sniffled their way around, snouting up clouds of sand they didn't realise that they were fishing right next to Marcia and Marvin.

Well, within seconds, we heard a deep pitched wail, like a fog horn with a cold - a combination of howl and scream - it was Hazel, she was beside herself.

Crying and thrashing around, her octopus ink eye shadow flowed like rivers down her face.

'You traitors' she sobbed. 'After all I have done for you, one bad cockle day and you sell yourselves to Marvin and his live in tart!!' She was really hurting.

Everyone was shocked into silence. Until Buster said 'don't you dare say that to me'. He then proceeded to tell Hazel a few home truths.

And then Jane, yes, jolly old Jane, joined in and gave her two flipper's worth and once she got going there was no stopping her. Buster was blasted and hard nut Hazel's reputation was hammered until it cracked.

It was as though the demons of the deep had been bottled up for years and someone had taken the cork out. Flipper swam away quietly, before he had a migraine, and the entire Pod separated off into threes and fours. What an awful day.

Dorcas nuzzled up to Grumpus and asked 'did they tell you anything about this at the University of Atlantis?'

'Well,' said Grumpus, 'one delegate did tell the story of the Tory

Party when John Major was running out of steam, and into hot water with Edwina - a Cabinet Minister with a late night chat show - and another Minister with glasses who had a problem with an orange - but nothing as bad as this'.

Then Grumpus said, 'I think I remember something that my Grand-dad told me about a fiasco off San Diego when new dolphins joined the Pod.

I'll need to poke my memory banks with a stick. But I will have to lie down first. Then I'll nip off to the Salmon's Leap, sit myself in a quiet corner with a half bottle and see what I can remember.'

Flipper thought – thousands of years of learning from what works, and learning more from the pain of what doesn't work – but we needed new knowledge or information to deal with today.

Grumpus is the source of all old knowledge. When he trawls his memory banks he will come up with something.

If I summarise the issues really well, we can accurately engage and connect with the right solutions, we can help Grumpus describe them.

Flipper summarised as follows;

Long term work systems and leadership patterns were being questioned.

Hazel thought that her knowledge, influence and ability to lead was being challenged. When she heard Pod members questioning - 'does she still have the right skills set'? She was really worried.

When the challenge came Hazel had responded aggressively and wound everybody up as she did.

50

Yesterday's problems change a little when a new dawn breaks

Dorcas, Grumpus, Flipper and Jess all had a restless night and to a mammal they all woke up at three in the morning, tossed, turned, yawned at themselves, but no one slept very well.

Poor Hazel hardly slept a wink. She was distraught, and had sobbed quietly most of the night - sniffed loudly in between sobs - and of course had a night long chat with the mind monster.

At one time there were six different thoughts orbiting in her head. Each one with a voice saying; how could she say that to you - you should do the following - if only you hadn't said this - you could of course have done that - and eventually her Grandmother - who had died many years earlier was in on the chat and giving her advice too.

As the sun rose it sent long light streams across the water and Hazel slept for ten minutes before she woke again knowing that she needed help and guidance as to how to tackle this new day.

Grumpus woke up in a quandary too, but his was different. He couldn't even open his eyes, the half bottle had become a whole bottle, and he thinks he moved on to the shorts, those sandquila snifters are deadly.

As he slept, like a walrus on a sunny rock, his old mind kept on sifting and analysing through the sands of time. Years of old memory, sense checked as he snored.

Flipper wrote down what Grumpus had remembered, just in case he forgot it again. It was a San Francisco fiasco and not a San Diego story, I knew it began with S', said Grumpus.

51

An established Pod had been fishing the same coastline for many years.

They were thirty strong, and had worked in teams of seven or eight, each team had an elder - a Lead dolphin.

This pods team rules were similar to ours, and they worked very well, anyone led on the first fish. On fish two, an elder stopped fishing and started Coordinating. Everything went swimmingly until the US Navy moved in on the pod.

They arrived armed with the bright idea that the Pod could be trained to plant magnetic mines on Japanese boats. Two big male dolphins - called Star and Stripes - explained the plan and then started to tell everyone what do.

Confusion followed. **If you want to confuse try changing the rules!**

The new guys broke all the Pod rules, said that there was a new way of working - with only one Leader - Sergeant Stripes - and the rest could do as they were told.

They swam around and around barking instead of squeaking and ignored the Pod rules on work system and Communication.

Chattering was to stop.

They themselves were incapable of listening, and they interrupted everyone so that they could repeat what they had said before.

Everyone lost heart and silent resistance grew.

No one called fish at any o'clock, and what had once been a really good and effective fishing team was now a gang of increasingly stubborn individuals.

52

One thing was for sure, Chattering never stops. We dolphins have been texting each other for ever, so low volume messaging continued.

The elders swam close together as the whole Pod nuzzled the sand banks, and they quietly evolved a plan as to how they could make these new ideas fail.

The new bods in the Pod made everyone close ranks.

Most of us kept a polite distance from Star and Stripes except that is for Simon. He thought Star was a real hero and he listened to his stories and plans on the new way for dolphins to change the world.

We were to work with just one leader and as one big Pod. Two corporals were to be announced at the pre-fish briefing.

Star was an obvious candidate with Jacob, Mary, Joseph and Daniel - the four Pod elders - the obvious short list for the second positions.

Well, when Star announced Simon as the second corporal there was uproar, 'what does he know', said Daniel as everyone chattered, 'he's dry behind the ears. He couldn't catch a cuttlefish in a pirate's locker'.

The four elders wanted to vote for a withdrawal of flippers. Star screamed 'you can't go on strike in the Navy'. Every one screeched right back but louder 'we are not in the f f f f fishing Navy.' The noise went on for days and even the whales detoured via Hawaii to avoid the din.'

'You see Jess the fact is that if you try and change an established Pod - introduce new rules, alter the way of working or organising, mess with existing lines of communication, or introduce new leaders then **this is tsunami time'.**

Any one of these changes will create a really big wave and when a number of changes combine, take the boats off the beach and practise hill running. There is a big emotional surge wave just about to hit the shore.

In San Fransico - things got physical.

Jacob who had flipper wrists like tree trunks - built up over years and years of pulling fishing nets off the back of boats and coiling them up at the bottom of the sea- felt the need to exercise his power.

And when Star tried to push his ideas with his tail Jacob delivered a mighty thwack across his ear.

Mary head butted Stripes until he had a few more - stripes that is - older dolphins can be very aggressive when needed. They can even fight off a shark and when the whole Pod turned on the Navy boys they left in a hurry singing 'we are sailing, we are sailing, stormy waters, head for home' to tune in the Chief of Staff for Navy Seals and Dolphins.

You see you can't change an existing order easily and when the Pod held a lessons-learned session they concluded that someone could have been hurt through their behaviour.

And that they had to agree new rules of engagement, before the Navy came back with re-inforcements.

Many of the Pod were unhappy with the way they had behaved under pressure and now was the time to set new rules for these circumstances, and for the next time.

Grumpus was asked to write a summary on no more than four pieces of sea weed for everyone to consider.

This was the Grumpus summary;

Before you introduce a new way, be sure you understand the old way.

Long term teams and organisations have predictable work systems - these are the ways of working - that people are comfortable with.

Pods and teams have established and powerful opinion leaders.

Everyone looks for guidance from these local and often informal leaders.

Informal leaders enjoy their status and power within the group, and Melvin is a good example. He is a really strong character at work, but he doesn't get to talk at all at home. Her indoors is a powerful woman - so work status is his only status - and he defends aggressively against any real or even imagined challenge to his personal power.

In Uh Oh time the whole team becomes defensive.

And if an outsider rumbles an existing leader, Pod instability always follows.

A Pods group-think and rules can usually be explained within the small teams. But very few teams actually relate the same story.

And we get spooked, frightened and confused by imposed changes. If an outsider says we can't, then we automatically think - Oh yes we can'. If they say we should, and the old lags say we shouldn't, then we don't.

When change arrives, the people with the power take the biggest hit, they are the leaders of the old order and have most to lose - influence, authority, face and grace – could be lost and this becomes a real worry.

The way that you introduce new ideas and change, really is important, and if you haven't pre planned how you will deal with a power shift - then just expect a bumpy ride.

Nominate someone in the Pod to call a time out if someone is behaving badly.

The San Francisco Pod hadn't really planned to batter the big fish from the Navy. Or to use the descriptive language - that they didn't want the shrimps to hear.

When a team is confused and stressed, reflect on the formula that has worked in the past.

We are a nice friendly Pod, and in future we will behave that way.

We need to have a Common Understanding on what is important to us.

*What do we value**; trust – respect – loyalty – looking after each other**, and recognise that in a high performance Pod, we expect these values to surface as behaviours even on a bad day.*

Looking after each other is the most important thing that we can do.

When an existing organisation has a new Leader- Wobbles RUS.

Stars and Stripes tried to initiate a change through pressure and fear- this was not going to work.

Short term, many of us just put our heads in the sand thinking - this will go away.

Wobbles, uncertainty, confusion, grew into deep rooted fear and when it does the old order always strikes back.

We can learn the lessons from yesterday and build a better foundation for decisions that we need to make today.

These pages are for your notes

List the reactions that you and your work team experience when someone or something new impacts on your working life.

Keep this simple - one comment - on one post it

Back at Cromarty Bay Jess has more questions

'Good morning Flipper' said Jess, 'I am pleased to see you. That was a real to do yesterday. Is Hazel OK, and why didn't anyone follow the bump thud, bump thud, this morning. Are they expecting after shocks?'

'Jess, good question, you are on form', said Flipper.

'Hazel is very quiet, she didn't sleep that well, none of us did really and no one was up to a spurt after the boat this morning. Little bit subdued is the summary to date, and Grumpus has a hangover - again - but he has come up with a few gems'.

'You see Jess it doesn't take much to upset a team, especially a long standing team, and yesterday's event all kicked off when Marvin said lets go left and Hazel wanted to go right. It wasn't an important decision, but Hazel thought that Marvin was challenging her role as the cockle hunt leader and when anyone's power base is challenged-they react.

Now I must say I haven't taken to Marvin. He's a slimy little git and I will splash sand in his eyes if he keeps muzzling Marcia in public. But the poor boy didn't mean to start World War three, or cause Hazel to remind everyone of everything bad that had happened in the last twenty years.

Hazel had off loaded more than she should have and whilst most of it was true, she isn't proud of what she said. Dorcas and Grumpus are going to have a word.

Grumpus's Granddad had told him a story about what happens when new leaders or new group members arrive in the Pod and he has a good analysis of what went wrong.

This will be an useful start point for describing how we put it right'.

'But Flipper' said Jess pointedly, 'this might have started off as Hazel describing something that wasn't really there, or making a problem out of a non issue, but the whole Pod has reacted.

Dorcas says that you could cut the atmosphere with a razor clam shell and that you wouldn't think that you were a team at all. The buzz has gone, and the chatter with it, even the lobsters were laughing at you. What do you plan to do?'

Flipper thought silently for what seemed like an age as he dredged through his memory, until Jess prompted him again by saying, 'Granddad says that when times are hard and problems difficult, we should think about what worked well, the last time we had a similar problem. What was working well before this circumstance arose?

Turn negative emotions into thought bubbles, pop each bubble with a pin, and ask what have we learned? Then instead of disintegrating as a Pod and a team, think about the formulae and the recipe that made you the best Pod in the Cromarty Firth'.

'Describe what works,' said Jess.

'Jess, you are a gem', said Flipper and he swam off to meet with the others, or at least round up the others. He felt like a sheep dog herding geese, his close knit team was spread far and wide and as he met each one, he asked them to start Chattering again and to send the message that they would meet at the Sutors - two big headlands that marked the entrance into the Cromarty Firth - at three o'clock when the tide was full in.

But first he met up with Grumpus and Dorcas and they ate a few prawns together and built on Grumpus's understanding of what had gone wrong off San Francisco and Dorcas's recall of what went right in Cromarty.

For each negative or problem, they exchanged ideas and then described a solution.

Converting shouldn'ts and mustn'ts and cant's into how we cans.

Dorcas repeated the strap-line from the Pilchard factory. **'Success comes in cans not in can'ts'** she said.

And together they described what had been good, and productive, and effective within their recall of their Pod's history.

They found that there was much more in the rights column than in the wrongs corner. And they described what they thought could work.

Jess was having her lunch when a great spray of water came straight through the window. 'Oh no, not another war' she thought, but it was Flipper, 'can you Skype your Granddad and organise a conference call' he asked, 'will do' said Jess, 'we'll meet here in five minutes, bring your headphones'.

So the bright young girl, and the smartest young dolphin, and Dorcas the enlightened middle aged mammal, talked their ideas through with the two wrinklies. Jess said that Grumpus's skin was much smoother than her Granddad's, but this was not unexpected in one so old.

Success comes in Cans

Flipper gave *'Success comes in cans not in cant's'* as the theme for the dialogue.

Each person talked for three minutes about what worked well – pre bang.

They described success, and recalled the way that they delivered results before Hazel went nuts.

It took an hour of deep listening and ideas exchange before they described a Common Purpose and a Way Forward.

Granddad then asked everyone to press the pause button.

He said 'This was the easy part, a small team describing success. What process do we follow to have the whole Pod describe success?

It's our job as the Leaders to help every dolphin describe a new way – we can give them a starter for ten - and then each team can describe their own success formula.

And I think we should invite the Orkney pod to join the dialogue. Then we'll have the same understanding when we need others to fish with us.'

They tested the core ideas on Hazel, Marcia and John the Bapfish.

Flipper invited the Orcadians to the three o'clock meet. Hazel and Marcia presented the ideas to the big team.

Then they chunked down into six - five dolphin - squads, all of the squads presented their ideas, and we described what success looked like. We retained much of the old but described more that was new.

Hazel eventually summarised everything on two flip charts and we created a small wave right across the Firth, when everyone clapped enthusiastically.

Hazel said, 'Yesterday had been awful, but today was a good day, we had ended up with a much better plan, smiles all around'.

You learn most when you implement a plan

'Does anyone have any concerns that we need to address or consider before we roll out the plan?' asked Granddad. 'Yes said Grumpus but I need to tell you a story.

When a few of the bods from the Pod and I were on tour off Oban last summer we bumped into - well almost - the one hundred meter long shark that I had seen before.

And yes, it was a submarine, but it did have green eyes and a window in the back with a box of Kleenex tissues in a fancy white sleeve, and five nodding dogs on the back sill.

As the sub moved with the waves, the dogs nodded, and this memory made me think about the meeting at Sutors Rock. All thirty dolphins had ended up going with the flow and nodded in harmony at the new plan.'

'Now think on', said Grumpus, 'A few days earlier, everyone was at war. Many old sores opened and to our knowledge none settled. Could one evangelic event close down all of that open hostility?'

Sure enough Grumpus's grey matter was working well and Granddad suggested that we do nothing in the short term other than *listen* to the Chatter - - and especially - *to what Pod members said first- when they discussed the plan and the way forward*.

And of equal importance 'what did Pod members **behaviour communicate** about their commitment to the implementation of the new plan?'

The most likely early hiccup factor, was the new rule on direction finding in the cockle bank. We had agreed that Hazel would lead the way in the first instance - and that anyone who had a Plan B would be able to call a time out and explain to everyone why they thought Plan A wouldn't work - and why Plan B was needed. If someone had a Plan C then this was aired too and then Dorcas would choose one plan, and we'd all follow.

Now we always ate cockles on a Friday, fish suppers Monday through Thursday but on Friday we remembered the patron Saint of Fishermen and combed for cockles.

Hazel led and went the same way as usual and the anti squad chatter started before we had even arrived. 'I knew this wouldn't work', said one, 'she'll never change' said another, 'I'm saying nothing' said Marcia and then she barked, 'Marvin put your head in the sand and keep sucking'.

Granddad had warned that whenever you empower teams and give them the freedom to work to a plan, old and new tensions arise.

Why does Dorcas have to decide what we do?
What about our TUNA rep? [Tuna United will Never Auto pilot]. What does she have to say about this?

There was so much noise and anti chatter that doing nothing was not going to work, we needed another Exec conference call and quickly.

Jess organised the conference call and they analysed what was working well. Everyone on line had three minutes to describe successes and then three minutes each on - what we could improve on.

What worked reviews first and then - what wasn't working as well as we expected. Safety was our first review – then we moved on to other headings like; direction finding on the cockle bank.

We actually shared great success on the model - Plan A or B, everyone listening in - Dorcas deciding the best plan to follow.

There were a few mutterings, but we were finding more cockles and we had actually used five different options - in what turned out to be the most successful day that anyone could remember.

The TUNA rep had been vocal. She thought that the speed at which we were picking cockles could result in back strain.

Everyone thought, well she would, wouldn't she. But we had noticed that Jane was jiggling down instead of bending from the hips, so listening to the TUNA rep was a genuine positive too.

Marvin hadn't said a word but he didn't really need to. He had that flat fish look on his face, even when his mouth wasn't full of sand, he just wasn't himself.

And unusually he hadn't come up with any alternative plans. In the end of fishing debrief, he was just dumb and silent.

'What has worked well today', said Dorcas with flipper raised at the white board. No one spoke so Dorcas wrote - **Best catch anyone can remember**. 'Were there any Safety issues or near misses today?' silence followed.

Worst of all, when she asked, 'Was everyone happy with today and then, are you looking forward to tomorrow?' Everyone had nodded.

Jess was really puzzled, best day ever on the cockle bank and the team still had the glums.

What was going on, answers on a post card please or e-mail to Don't know.com.

You might want to write your recap thoughts here.

- Confusion
- Uncertainty
- Big emotional hits

Are stepping stones to a new and better way of working

When a team is confused, really worried team members often resort to old behaviour patterns called games

The Games that dolphins play

Grumpus retold another story from the fishing banks off California where his ancestors had first heard the stories and messages from a fisherman called Eric Berne who had written a book called Games People Play.

As they listened to the fisherman's tale they couldn't really believe that humans would be that stupid.

But there again, they were in the middle of melting the ice cap at the North pole, best leave the jury out at this time!

Anyway, in simple speak, old Eric said that humans often don't mean what they say and that words and messages can be a stepping stone to a bigger and grander plan.

So when Marvin gave Marcia a mussel and admired her tail fin this could all be a game leading up to the real question - what about a twitter patter?

Granddad has described more of the Games that People Play on page 155, but we only need to explore a few of them at this point in our story. We will try to explain how the game works through a dolphin example, the game is called NIGYSOB- *now I've got you, you son of a barnacle.*

Grumpus had watched Jane play this game on Hazel the day before yesterday and to understand the recent story he needed to reveal the sub plot and its history.

In the old days, jolly Jane was the Vice President of the Ancient Order of Cockle pickers. That is until the University of Atlantis opened up and Hazel and others, studied ultrasonic cockle finding.

Jane had argued against the new way until she was blue in the gills. 'This will not work', she huffed.

Well it did work and Jane was voted off the Governing body. She has never forgiven the whole of the cockle picking world for this rough justice, and has always blamed Hazel for her demise.

Now this was all a very long time ago and everyone thought it was forgotten until Marvin stirred up the mud with Marcia and Jane had decided to give Hazel the tongue bashing.

Years of venom poured out of her mouth and when she was heard to call Hazel - *a son of a barnacle* - the ultimate insult - everyone recognised that there was a much deeper underlying script at work than today's issue. This was not about, how do we find cockles or any other today issue. An old score had become confused with today's agenda.

Jolly Jane had smouldered through what she considered as injustice for years and years and this was payback time - *NIGYSOB - now I've got you, you son of a barnacle.*

Granddad says that resistance to change doesn't surface until you do something. And that this usually displays in undercover actions as opposed to open exchanges.

At the team debrief, no one says what most people think - this a load of old cockle shells - they say nothing, or at the very worst they just nod.

This game has been described as *NoDS the Nodding Dog Squad* and if you read between the lines you'll realise why we may not see many of this breed at Crufts or anywhere at all really.

The following is a true story. The Company leaders were briefing the plan as to how they thought they could save the Company from closure.

Everyone sat through the meetings and nodded. A significant majority made supportive noises when the dialogue moved to one to one discussions.

Now the reason that there is no future for the Nodding Dog breed is that not one of them had the balls to stand up and say in public what they were thinking and saying in private.

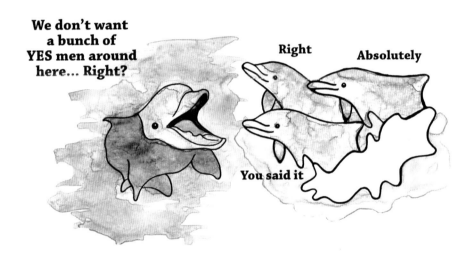

Even worse, having nodded through the plan and failed to come up with workable alternative ideas, small groups actually sabotaged the plan with local self interest power plays.

These games resulted in seven hundred people losing their jobs.

How stupid was that? We think they might have employed too many sharks and not enough dolphins.

Through open debate, and the discussion of very different opinions they could have made progress, through covert games they lost everything.

And next up came - the blame game – *WCWBFthis - Who Can We Blame for this -* A game for dumb losers.

Dumb because they don't want to learn or even consider how they could change to avoid a repeat of past problems or failures.

Losers - because as soon as they pin the tail on the blame donkey - they really do believe that they are relieved of all responsibility.

> What should *I do differently* doesn't figure because *they* - someone else that is - are the problem. I don't need to do anything until *they do something different*.

In the true story described above - *Who can we blame for this -* then took over.

The Company blamed the National Officer of the Union, and the problem of working with ex dock workers in the Tentacle & Gravallax Union.

And the Union blamed the Company for deliberately fabricating a loss making formulae to close the facility.

Neither of these logics were true but as both power broker groups dug deeper holes and threw sand grenades at each other, they openly described **'the others, as the real problem'**. **They** were the real reason for the lack of progress.

Who can we blame for this – the answer was the other party. A well paid working community died.

The end was quick, jobs lost in an eye blink, when the new Company owner decided to - close the facilities - with the biggest problems.

This facility had really good workers. Everyone said that they delivered the best quality and the best service. How on earth did this work place become consigned to the good old days in the minds of its former workers?

Granddad said it was because they didn't understand the power of the *BATNA* first described by a distant relative of yours - a fisherman.

Roger the Fisher man says that 'whoever has the
***Best Alternative To a Negotiated Agreement* will ultimately
win** – in the event of no agreement and a stand off.

The person or team that has the power to walk away from a negotiation, and lose the least, always wins. Where there is no agreement, they have the better alternative' - BATNA.

Grandad then told more of the true story - of the games that had been played - and the logics that had evolved over twenty years of work at the facility.

The root of the problem was that the Leaders in the Management and the Union had been around for so long that they thought like dinosaurs.

Very predictable game lines were drawn. 'Go and No go', and 'We do and We don't - on both sides, had created long term and fixed behaviour patterns.

For example, the company had become very successful; they were handling more and more work.

Customer demands were increasing. And they now needed to change shift patterns. The company needed; twenty four hours a day, seven days a week service and therefore more people to work weekends. But no one wanted to change shift.

This hassle had gone on for years, with a local Management – Union head butting contest roughly every six weeks. With two big bang butt sessions before Easter and Christmas every year. The Union had the short term *BATNA*, as they took up their usual positions for the head butt challenge - 'if you change our shift patterns, we will go on strike'.

This gave the Management a real headache, so they sat in small dark rooms, moved work to other facilities to reduce overtime and increase Colleague pain.

They called in the Lawyers to make sure they were legal, and arm wrestled each other to show how strong they were.

Directosaurus was the Management's Leader. A big hitter carrying an awful lot of clout and he was to pit his power and wit against Stewardorex the Union leader - in the final show down.

On fight night, they met at the Madjedski amphitheatre in Reading, the whole arena fell silent, the atmosphere was charged, tense but hushed.

Directosaurus crouched in Sumo position as did Stewardorex. They both broke stance, threw salt into the air, and pumped up their supporters as they swung left and then right and then thuderation - one almighty head butt left them both flat on the ground - centre stage.

Their supporters rushed in with damp towels and they all agreed that they should recess until after Easter.

They limped home to the sound of jungle drums, the Management drums said 'We won, boom boom, we won', and the Union drum said, 'We won, boom bang bang, we won'.

This was a twice a year ritual for the big guys, but the spin off Games at local level were of Olympic proportions.

You needed real stamina for this contest, meeting after meeting, routine crises on the night shift and on most weekends.

'The boys are not happy; morale is the worst it's ever been'. People behaved badly, just because they had the short term *BATNA.*

Just say no, was the dish of the day - whatever they ask you to do - *Just say No*.

And as the tribes belief in their power grew so did the games, *WOTNOBs* was next. *We are not talking to you because.*

You are not in procedure, or we do not recognise your job title, or you failed to bring one of our Stewards back from nights, or our Senior Rep is sick.

And a routine, cover all classic - we do not agree with the minutes that we signed off at the end of the last meeting.

Any one of these and many others came into the *WOTNOB* category; *We Are Not Talking to you today Because.*

But the Fisher man was right. At the end the Management had the most powerful long term *BATNA*. More powerful than the Union *BATNA* .

Neither Management nor Union were right but power prevailed. Management joined the - *Just say No* lobby - no more work for you that is.

How many innocents lose their jobs and livelihoods when the big boys play games?

And what about the Bush – Blair – Iraq affair?

Saddam refusing entry to Inspectors - that he knew wouldn't find any weapons anyway.

His WOTNOB's game - we *are not talking to you* ended up with him hanging from a rope.

Bush was the boy with the *BATNA* and he really did get himself a cowboy, but one who didn't have the weapons to bomb London.

Four thousand armed forces died in Iraq in the first five years - why?

And how many mothers and children lose their lives when the Dinosaurs play Games?

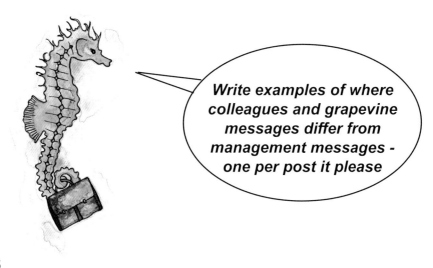

Write examples of where colleagues and grapevine messages differ from management messages - one per post it please

76

As the stories unfolded we named our games

'Hey Granddad that was a deep dive' said Grumpus, 'that story makes a fight on the cockle bank sound like chicken sh…, oops sorry Jess.'

'Well wash your mouth out with soapy water' said Jess with an American accent - 'my friend is from the US of A and we have trouble with bullies at school, and come to think of it, we play quite a few mind games.

We play Name games like, we don't like her, and sometimes we have a meet in the corner and decide that - she is not going to be our friend, and - he is not coming to my party.

One girl has a hit list that records I don't like him or her, and they are really awful. Getting listed isn't difficult with even - her mother said to my mother - as a reason for escalation to the naughty list.

'There is no one worse at playing Games than us dolphins, said Dorcas. The whole Pod plays *MyGang* if you are in our gang of five your opinion counts if you're not, forget it - talk to the flipper - cos the head ain't listening.'

'And, *GATME Gospel According To Me* - there is only one way to do this and it's my way. And we are always on standby for one of Hazel's famous huffs when we don't conform to her script.'

'What about *KIPPERS'* said Grumpus, '*Knowledge Is Power People Expecting Ransoms?* You remember the story of the Navy bods who wanted us to plant mines on the hulls of Japanese ships. Well, they had the bright idea but they didn't know how to do it.

Star and Stripes called a strategy Conference, or so they said, with Sammy the celebrity seal as the warm up act. He had a ball on his nose, he threw it to Star who threw it back to Sammy, who nodded the ball back to Star, to me - to you - to me. The sea horse said, 'what a one trick pony'.

Star pumped it up 'Wow' he cheered and clapped and Stripes said 'Go Star, Go Sam, good job!' And we all thought - good for making you dizzy perhaps.

Then they announced small conference room groups to discuss different ways of pushing the mines through the water.

Now most of us knew exactly what we needed to do. We had been pushing lobster pots around for years and we had even salvaged a whole cargo container of tinned salmon - opening each tin with a stick.

We could have picked up the mine, nosed it on to the hull and triggered the timer with a twig if we had wanted to.

Fact was we weren't interested in these Navy outsiders or their magnet mine munitions. Our knowledge was our power so we just *KIPPER'd* and told them nothing.

Naming the game reveals the underlying script

'When people play games, are they really living in a make believe world'? Asked Jess.

'I think they are' said Grumpus, 'When we played games with Star and Stripes they turned all sorts of tricks and tactics to find the answer. Subtlety at first, then they tried to bully us.

Fact is that when an outsider to our group arrives and asks questions, we automatically think - there is something fishy going on here. So we help create a fantasy world for them to live in.'

78

Whenever somebody new arrives we tell them nothing - of substance that is. We play *NKOTB - New Kid On the Block* and if we have to answer questions we either give them *DUFINFO- duff information,* or if we take an instant dislike to them - *we don't tell them any thing at all - NOINFO.'*

'But what if they really have come to help' asked Granddad.

'Well how would we know' said Grumpus,' They all say I'm from Head office and I'm here to help you, and as far as we were concerned we didn't need any help at all, thanks very much.

You see no one really knows what goes on down here except us and when the next change missionary arrives - they usually come with a re-package of the same old smelly fish heads as the last lot.

Most of their opening spiel fast tracks us to - we have been here before - this is the same as - and then someone always takes us off message with an old war story.

Do you remember when the last but one Pod leader arrived? She had followed a sprat boat up from Italy. Told us we were rubbish and that we would be blocked out of the Firth if we didn't change with the times.'

This was exactly what the last outsider had told us.

She didn't last very long.

'What can we learn about what worked from the past, that helps us all create a better future?' Asked Granddad.

'Are there examples of someone arriving with information that you rejected, and it turned out to be true'?

'Yes there is,' said Dorcas. 'A really flashy Sea Horse arrived carrying a brief case. He was tall and had really lovely deep, deep, blue eyes.

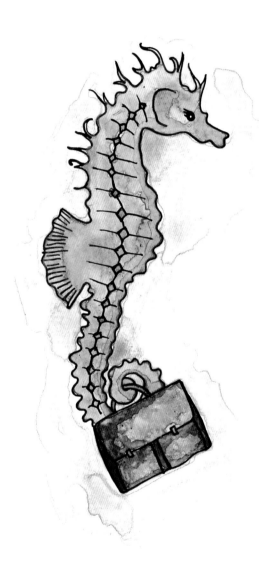

Hazel took an instant dislike, 'you can never trust the flashy good looking ones' she said. 'Just look at him, he thinks he's the answer to every jelly fish's prayer.'

'I liked him, but none of the male mammals liked him either, and when he told us that 'big boys were going to dig an enormous hole and then concrete over one of the cockle beds, we thought he's having a laugh'.

There we were fifty miles from anything bigger than a small village, and their cement mixer could only churn out concrete blocks.

The whole Pod gave him a rough ride. This one and then that one asked him question after question to the point where he was lobster pink.

I said, 'Well, what if he is right?'

If I did, everyone aimed all the questions at me. And when Hazel said, we know you have a soft spot for blue eyes and that I'd be better off swimming with the prawns, she made me feel very small. I wouldn't do that again.

The Sea Horse galloped off.

'I always remember his wavy blond hair and his Public school accent long after I had forgotten most of what he had said.'

As a matter of fact every one of us had forgotten what he had said until the day we heard an unusual bump noise. It sounded like; bump thud grind squeak, bump thud grind squeak. The distant sound got louder and seemed to be closing in on us, eventually it went right over our heads and into the Cromarty Firth.

Within minutes we heard the screams. There were cockle tears everywhere, the grind turned out to be a dredging machine that gobbled up huge chunks of sand and then vomited them into the bowels of a big flat barge. The barge, when full, was towed away and the contents dumped into the deepest sea.

And the cockles went too, day after day, barge after barge, for months, until they had a hole that was deeper than the Firth itself.

We were really worried. No one could figure out why the whole of the sea wouldn't disappear into the hole. And then it got worse, they filled the hole with smelly white stuff that turned really hard. Then they moved in the noisiest machines that we had ever heard. There were bright eerie lights at night with smoke trails drifting upwards into the night sky.

Grumpus was convinced that they were making another enormous grey metal shark.

Well, it turned out to be an oil rig yard. The Sea horse had been right, but we hadn't listened to him.

That is, no one except me, I had listened to every word - he had really nice teeth. Always an asset to a horse, don't you think?'

Grumpus summarised by saying. 'We just don't trust newcomer's messages or their motives. The voice of experience to date says that they are more interested in themselves and their careers, and their bonus than in us.

They come, and they go, tide comes in, tide goes out. And until they understand what is important to us, they will not be able to influence us'.

No matter who they are, 'until we invite them in to our world - they stay out – they will not be listened to - they will not be able to influence us.'

'Granddad, do you have a list of games that you understand, that help you interpret behaviour,' asked Jess.

'Yes I do' said Granddad 'but Eric Berne and other Wrinklies can describe even more.

Using the metaphor or telling the story sometimes helps other people identify and connect with the underlying messages'.

These are work in progress summaries

NIGYSOB now I've got you, you son of a bitch [or barnacle]
You've done something to hurt me and this is my chance to get even.

NoDS the nodding dog squad
I don't agree with this but I will nod, say nothing, and do the opposite.

WCWBFthis - who can we blame for this
A reason to do nothing, it's their fault, hand washing time. And for as long as I can muster support for describing someone else as the real problem, I don't need to do anything.

BATNA best alternative to a negotiated agreement
When you fail to reach agreement, the power of the what next - alternative, wins the day. Companies can always build powerful long term alternatives. Union leaders often over use short term *BATNA's.*

I can't think of a more up to date *BATNA* than the Bushman in Iraq.

WOTNOBS we are not talking to you today because
When the organisation moves into a play games mode. Meetings are cancelled, deadlines missed and a whole raft of spurious reasons for not behaving normally are exchanged.

Grown men and women peddle trivia as reasons why they can't. Attacks on the other side become personal, hurtful and bitchy.

MYGANG my gang
You're OK if you fit in with us. Starts in our schools, extends to sports teams, street gangs, churches, social groupings, towns and then nations.

GATMe The gospel according to Me
One really good Union Colleague christened a Leader as Frank Sinatra, 'but he can only sing one song and that's - My Way.... I did it my way'.

My gang rules are usually described by powerful local Leaders who set the rules and boundaries through *GATMe*. Standby for trouble if you try to work outside these tribal laws.

Senior Managers sometimes have a problem even talking to lower level employees.

Similarly most Union members will vote in favour of electric shock therapy to Noners - Workmates who haven't joined the Union - when GATME reigns.

KIPPERS knowledge is power people expecting ransoms - If I don't tell you what I know I'm safe.

You can't work without me or you have to ask me to come to work on overtime because only I have this knowledge.

At worst the machine malfunctions at the start of the next shift requiring the recall of the man who fixed it last.

He was then paid eight hours and a callout payment for an hours work, and this to include twenty minutes spent looking for the parts in his tool bag, in the canteen.

KIPPERS believe it's their right to hold to ransom - pay packets always large and handsome.

With equal gravitas Managers fix things, to rounds of corporate applause when they shouldn't have even happened in the first place. Management incompetence causes the routine fires that they then become expert at putting out.

84

NKOTB new kid - or even a new data system - on the block- New Leader, new role and in general anyone that needs to break into the old membership circle triggers abnormal behaviour. There may be a honeymoon period of days or months, but all old Empires strike back.

From childhood, we grow to love what we know and are familiar and at ease with. Organisations stitch a protective patchwork blanket to extend over their comfort zones. These can be five, ten or thirty years old, and as long as the environment in which they were created doesn't change, then things can work OK underneath them.

The older the organisation, the more stable and predictable the way people work, then the greater the resistance to change when it arrives.

It's in the nature of man to work at things until they become easier. As work time passes, Managers and Support staff in particular can make them selves real work redundant.

But no one else knows. They attend meetings, conform to group rules, tick all the boxes and since the advent of the desk top computer they can now practice hypnosis on a screen.

No one in this world knows that they are doing, not a lot in a week, or even a year.

Clock up long hours, do next to nothing, add little or no real value, but say yes and always, always nod - ho hum - no one need know.

Except themselves that is, and for as long as they can operate in steady mode the world of work is a very comfortable and a great place to be.

Then; when the new manager - or budget - or data network - or Consultant [often considered as a wart on the body Corporate] - or any other outsider arrives. Mild and then escalating panic rumbles are felt by everyone.

With the biggest wobbles hosted by the ones who hold the - I do not do a lot in a year for my money - secret.

And when 'What if' the mind monster leaves its cage - and runs riot at all times of the night, the sleep less worrier talks to it and feeds it buns to make it go away.

No one knows better than we do if we are under performing or not adding value.

'What if - they find out'? This is the mind monster's repeated question.

Whatever the Change factor is, be it; boss - new structure - budget - or reporting systems- fear will become the driver of abnormal behaviour.

Recruited into an Executive post, one change leader was desked at the far end of a busy open plan office.

The *MYGANG* squad took it in turn to move her chair, often to the other end of the office, every time she left it.

Forty people were too busy to notice that she was walking past, wheeling the chair back to her desk. They were screen gazing, but all broke set, to smile at each other after she had passed.

NOINFO or DUFFINFO no information or duff information

Established teams actually close out newcomers who do not have enough power, by telling them nothing. They deliberately exclude them from Information and Communication and even Chatter - *NOINFO*

This often escalates into giving them the wrong information. The Exec with the moving chair travelled to London for an every Thursday, order progress and performance meeting.

Tuesday and Wednesday were spent; checking,analysing and then signing off all of the plans and the delivery data before the London meeting. All of the information was well documented, with order status and commitments agreed.

When the new Leader presented the information at the London meeting it was contested by the Customer who had been given new information that very morning through the old guard network.

DUFFINFO is at its most dangerous when it exhibits with your Customers.

Name the games that your organisation plays

Big boys play World wide Games

American Foreign Policy decisions are littered with a combination of; *NOINFO, DUFFINFO, MYGANG,* and *GATME.* Irving Janis described this in his book entitled **Groupthink.**

From the American invasion of Cuba in 1961 to the basis on which we went to war with Iraq in 2003 there are frightening examples of world impact decisions, not being based on facts.

Janis interviewed close to one hundred decision makers in John F Kennedy's staff teams. Over ninety percent confessed to believing that the plan to invade Cuba would fail, before the invasion had even started.

The CIA were found to be guilty of; *NOINFO, DUFFINFO* with systematic exclusion through *MYGANG* of all alternative opinions. Everyone had nodded.

The plan that Kennedy had signed off - following advice from his Staff teams - was to land troops at night, move quickly to the mountains, arm the waiting local guerrilla armies, and they, when armed, would easily overthrow Castro.

American troops were to exit stage left, the very same night, quietly and quickly.

When the deed was done America was not to be seen to be pivotal to the outcome - thus minimising the risk of retaliation by the Russians.

But no one had mentioned the twenty miles of swamp that was likely to bog down all of the American landing craft and heavy armaments as soon as they left the beach.

The heavily flawed invasion plan failed, to Kennedy and America's great embarrassment.

Anyone who had wanted to explore an alternative plan had been branded as a Red under the bed. The power brokers deliberately and systematically blocked out alternative opinions, and this resulted in Kennedy not being given the facts.

Investigating North Korea, Vietnam and other American invasions, Janis described the exact same symptoms that some believe will become clear on the recent invasion of Iraq.

The power brokers went to war with their own introverted version of the facts. There were no weapons of mass destruction, only the footprints in the sand of where they might have been.

Iraq's Foreign Minister was christened the Minister for Mis-Information when he repeatedly said 'there are no weapons of mass destruction, you will find nothing'.

This said, Saddam had helped propagate the - we have the power myth - and hundreds of thousands of people died as he sabre rattled at the Bush man.

When the world plays covert games and doesn't deal in open facts, when decisions are left to local power brokers, history tells us that ordinary people lose.

The same Groupthink cliques manifest in school groups that become gangs and in other assorted tribes; sports, religious, political, all with their own views of the world - and through these narrow opinions they often build justifications - for doing whatever they like.

We do however have the opportunity to understand one set of facts in our work Organisations.

They are not too complex or difficult to understand. With the proviso that the organisation is mature enough to limit the extent to which people are allowed to play undercover games.

There will be reasons why the full facts of an invasion cannot be disclosed and the same applies to business issues. But is there any justification for proceeding with a plan, where people might be misled through the lack of genuine information.

In our business organisations, everyone is entitled to hear the facts, so that they can make an informed choice.

Unfortunately, power brokers tend to peddle only their own versions of the truth and market their views with mistrust messages. "Don't listen to them - listen to me" – and they often ignore the real facts of the situation.

In a low trust environment even the facts may not be listened to.

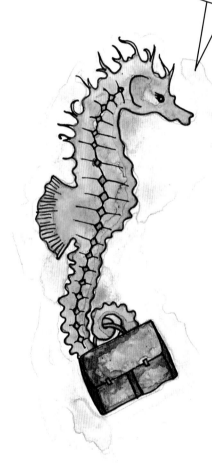

Could we have saved the cockles if we listened?

'Well yes, but not the cockle bed', said Flipper, 'The oil rig yard was coming anyway there was nothing that we could have done to stop it'.

'That's the way with environmental changes, when they impact it's often too late to do anything anyway' said Grumpus. 'What we could have done, if we had listened to Smarty-pants the sea horse, was to encourage the cockles to move to another bed.

But you know what they are like, real stick in the sands. When we asked them to think about moving last year, with a really good reason, they said they had heard it all before.

I met one of them at the University of Atlantis, a real hard case studying the life and times of the Brahan Seer from 1650 to the later part of that century.

Cameron the cockle had said - 'Kennoth Odhar, his Visionary hero had been born in Uig on the Isle of Lewis and had been gifted - with a little black stone with a hole, through which he could foresee the future - by his mother, who had had a night out on the spirits.

Many stories of his predictions and futuring were handed down from fire side Elders to Youngers and until1890 there were few written records.

And although the stories will have changed in the telling over hundreds of years, when they were eventually collated and written up, many of them had come true.

The power of these old messages and prophecies could even have impacted on our cockle bed - three hundred and thirty years after the story was first told.

This connection having been researched exclusively by Cameron - the new Cockle Futurist - as he was now to be known.

The Brahan Seer had said that there would be a one legged monster, breathing fire in the North Sea, and that when the ninth bridge was built over the River Ness, there would be fire and flood and calamity. The ninth bridge was duly built in 1987 and in 1988 the Piper Alpha rig - looking for all the world like a one legged monster - exploded, caught fire and killed 167 oil workers.

And just one year later in 1989 the rail bridge built in 1862 across the river Ness was washed away by a flood, and, and, said Grumpus, getting really excited as he related the story - the oil rig that caught fire had actually been built on the cockle bed, our cockle bed.

Our Firth has been the home of Visionaries for ages, and there are lessons to be learned.

Kennorth Odhar was re-named the Brahan Seer when his ability to; tell stories, find water, and predict the future - by looking through his stone - came to the notice of the local landowner the Earl of Seaforth. He employed him on his Brahan Estate as a labourer, sooth sayer, fortune teller, and futurist by appointment through the name the Brahan Seer.

And we have every reason to believe that he made lots of good judgement calls when the chattering classes asked him 'what should we be concentrating on today or thinking about tomorrow?'

He rightly predicted the place and outcome of the bloody Battle of Culloden, and the destruction by fire of nearby Fearn Abbey. He said that this would result from a lightning strike, and this actually came true in 1742. Unfortunately by this time poor Kennorth was long gone.

94

His good Lord Seaforth had been on an extended business trip in Paris and Isabella his wife routinely asked the Seer for news of his well being. She was dutifully informed that 'all with the good Lord was well'.

Problem was that the Lady wanted a more detailed and specific answer, and is rumoured to have enticed, cajoled and even bribed the man with the stone with a hole. She just wanted him to foretell what she wanted to hear - he could have made a mint.

And near to the end of his story, he did tell her what she had wanted to hear.

Once more she asked the oft repeated question - 'Was the good Lord twitter pattering with the natives in Paris?'

This time he answered-Yes-and added,'but everything is going to be all right, he's coming home to see you very soon and he will explain everything when he arrives'.

This was indeed another true prophecy. Within a week the Lord really was home.

But a week was a long time in the politics of the Black Isle. The good Lady had already gathered the Church and local dignitaries at the Monastery in Fortrose - for an anti social event.

She condemned poor Kennorth, arguing that he had been communing with the devil for far too long. He was consigned to die, head downwards in a barrel of burning tar, this being the local end-ritual for everyone convicted of witchcraft.

Lord Seaforth, arriving home with a really good story, was too late to convince his wife that the tale should have had a happier ending.

Fact is that when you describe the future and tell people what they don't really want to hear, you are living right on the edge of trouble and strife.

We were just about to tell the story telling Cockle to get a life when a Tuna tuned in and said, 'Its true, this story is true.'

At Chanonry point, right opposite where Jess lives is a plaque that marks the spot where the Brahan Seer was burned and his black ashes buried'.

'The past is useful' said Granddad, 'as long as it is used to inform the future'.

So if you find the stone with a hole, last seen sinking slowly into Loch Ussie, destined said the soon to die Seer, 'to be swallowed by a fish'. Another forecast from history will come true.

Now it doesn't matter where the story came from, if the cockles had known, that the one eyed monster was going to be built on their cockle bed they would have moved willingly.

We had all decided to ignore good Information and at grave cost.'

The power of vision

Flipper decided that we needed to learn the lessons from history, through accurate recordings, and from as factual a baseline as we could achieve.

The history of what works and what doesn't could then inform our next steps as we describe a way forward - Our Vision - should evolve into a go forward plan and result in fewer surprises.

'When the salmon count at Bonar Bridge fell from many thousands to low hundreds we were in trouble, we were not ready for this change'.

'The cockles were hanging on to the sand with their only tooth as the dredger dumped them on to the barges. Some said we shouldn't worry - the tide has gone out early - dig into the sand and everything will be all right. Next thing they knew they were rattling around in a giant cement mixer, minutes away from becoming concrete! Some dug deeper into the sand'.

'For most of our lives our Pod has been reacting to changes around us, knee jerking our way through one problem after another and mainly because we thought we had seen it all, and that we knew all the answers.'

'When the Sea horse said that we needed to change, most of us said that's a load of bull and some even said horse droppings. Then we were caught out again'.

Now Pliny the Elder said that we were the most intelligent animals on the planet and Kennorth the Seer said good things about us too. Fact is that we need to start describing our future, we can't leave it to chance.

We need to think through the what-ifs and plan to reduce the consequence of risks. We need to do this for our Pod and for the much bigger organisation that we work within.

We can't do this alone, we are part of an inter dependent eco system, prawns eat green bugs and so do little fish, and then mackerel eat little fish and everything else under the sea that moves. Then we eat the mackerel. The cockles gobble everything that's even smaller and we eat them too.

We need a plan that looks after our whole environment and outlines the way that we will work with each other and support one and another - over the longer term.

'Let's have an Ideathon at Sutors Rock and invite everyone".

'I'm not sure about that' said Grumpus ' That is exactly what Star and Stripes did off San Francisco, didn't work at all we *KIPPERED them.*

The principle is good but we need to give the process more structure and direction. Why don't we form a small Executive Team and describe 'Our Sea World in 2012' and then we convene the Ideathon with the purpose of building on the core ideas.

We can ask the bottom feeders to describe their future, invite; Cockles RUS, the Mackerel Preservation Society, the Lobster lobby, all describing conditions in their four meters of sea, whilst the Jelly fish and Basking sharks describe life at the top. Sea horses cover the fast lane and we dolphins describe wave tops to deep dives, and Oh yes - Tourism.

'Start chattering' said Dorcas, 'let everyone know we will meet for a conference in the river pool - at the Salvesen House, where Winston used to chill out, with a cigar on Church hill, during the war - in three weeks from now.

We'll present some initial ideas and then we need three movers and shakers from all of the inhabitants of the Cromarty and Moray firths. Everyone; seals to star fish, whales to whelks, to attend. They will listen to our start messages for describing 'Our Sea world in 2012' – and then we build on those ideas.'

'Will three weeks be enough for the Executive to do the work' asked Grumpus?

'If we say three months, it will take three months. We need a tight deadline and nominate people to the Exec who want to get on with it and deliver.'

And remember, the Exec will describe the big picture and longer term, just an overview.

We then engage the movers and shakers -the Opinion formers- from each representative group to add the detail', said Granddad.

'How will three to five members of each group be able to send the new message to hundreds and perhaps a thousand of their fish kin folk', asked Flipper.

'They won't' said Grumpus, 'the Exec will be responsible for taking the message right down to the sea bed'. Cascade doesn't work, the message doesn't get down to the worms, cockles and the other bottom workers on whom everyone's food chain depends.'

With the messages fresh in his mind from his fellow delegates at the University of Atlantis, Grumpus said, 'We don't need videos, or brochures or iffy slogans like - prawns are our biggest asset, or any other corporate bling. Simple messages and early direction are all we need to open up a genuine dialogue'.

'What's a dialogue', said Dorcas.

'An open exchange of ideas, shared between interested parties, who come together to offer their own thoughts and to listen to everyone else's,' said Granddad.

'This can be really powerful, providing that is, that no one swims in believing that they have the one and only answer'.

'I knew a dog fish just like that' said Dorcas, 'he used to head butt rocks in the hope that a fish would come out, some said he had a rock logic all of his own.

Every time we had a meeting, he had an opinion, on everything, and a long winded version at that. He usually left the meeting with- the idea that he came in with.

100

One wag called him a light house, said the 'light was always on but there was never anyone in'.

'We need to set the rules for dialogue' said Grumpus 'who are we going to nominate for the Executive?'

Jess said 'You can count me out, I don't know enough about life down there to be able to add real value'. 'Well Jess' said Flipper, 'I think you are right and you are wrong, as usual'.

'You are right, in that you can only view from the surface, with the exception of the occasional swim that is, but because **you don't know the detail or the history, you always add real value**.

You always ask the daft questions that often turn out to be the right questions. Who do you think we need on the Executive? What about Grumpus, and you Flipper, and you Dorcas and Tammy the Tuna rep' said Jess.

'Why have the Tuna rep ? asked Dorcas,' Because she brings in a different perspective' said Jess 'and she spends a lot of time with the shrimps, cockles, barnacles and whelks, and they are the biggest of all of the groups that we need to engage.

I would ask Tammy to nominate the movers and shakers from her groups, she knows them much better than we do', said Jess.

'Jess, you have done it again' said Flipper with a growing pride in his protégé, 'I don't know anyone who is as capable as you, or with such an ability to think outside the cockle shell'.

Jess asked her Granddad to talk to Grumpus and summarise the plan, Granddad talked, with Grumpus adding value;

Our Sea World in 2012, would evolve from an Executive team outline of a way forward for the organisation.

The executive summary would be reviewed and improved on by approximately twenty leaders representing all levels within the organisation, recognising that really efficient Pods work with very good local Leaders. These natural leaders are the best people to understand what really works and the important people to test the go-forward-ideas with.

Then we engage with between fifty and sixty Opinion formers, ideally the passionates about progress, like Hazel and Hamish, and even Doberman the dogfish, everyone's input and opinions needed'.

'Doberman!' exclaimed Grumpus 'are you having a laugh? You won't even get him to turn up, and if you do invite him he'll dominate the air time and talk the hind legs off the sea horse's cousin. You know the one with a cross on his back that says he-haw. He has more old war stories than a Chelsea pensioner'.

'We need him there and we need his input' said Granddad 'Better to have him voicing his opinions. He would add more value than others, who say nothing and then with equal rigour do nothing as well. I'm sure that Tammy the TUNA rep will want Dogma the other dogfish there. If we can align the problem fish with the rest of us, they will offer really good ideas.'

'Don't say I didn't warn you' said Grumpus.

'We can test the ideas with the Support team leaders, and then the Opinion formers and we incorporate their ideas into the plan, that we then roll out to everyone. And we leave enough design space in the plan for the input of every single team in the Firth'.

The Exec communicate the way forward, we engage the people that work along side us, they add value and when we roll out these ideas we invite everyone to improve on the core ' Our Sea World in 2012 messages'.

102

Jess to describe the rules for the dialogue

Round tables seating ten; one flip chart per table. All tables were to have; Exec, Support and Opinion former Leaders. Everyone understands that this is a first amongst equals dialogue. Role, rank, status, all left at the door, inputs valued, best thoughts to be communicated and adopted.

One Exec team member presents the core ideas to all of the assembled delegates describing 'Our Sea World 2012' and prescribes a series of headings for each round table to consider.

Each table nominates a Leader, an Appraiser and a Resource person. The Leader presents the table's output to the other delegates. The Appraiser helps keep the team on track and the discussion focused. Resource will help manage air time and everyone's engagement.

Jimwatt the kilted crayfish frae Govan will be Master of the house, facilitator of the dialogue, interpreter of all things Gaelic and give expert opinion on all references to the Brahan Seer.

Each table will communicate their thoughts and then everyone will be suitably occupied whilst the Exec summarise the interim dialogue outcomes.

We then form one large rectangular table that accommodates all delegates. Nominate a Leader, Appraiser and Resource for a further dialogue.

Everyone at the table has three minutes to present their own thoughts on 'Our Sea World 2012'

Then we summarise these outputs into one - Purpose message - that explains what we are trying to do. We invite every team in the Firth to adopt the Purpose and add value to the Plan.

Last but not least, every team communicates the support that it needs to be able to implement a 30-60-90 day action plan that aligns with the Purpose.

Support teams monitor progress against plan and the Exec review periodically, we keep it as simple as we can, and deliver on all of the local Plans.

Are your work Colleagues able to describe what they need to do to deliver your organisations Purpose?

Grumpus writes the guidelines for Action plans

It's the teams on the ground that will make a real difference. When they understand our Purpose they collect the performance data in their own work areas and we Support them in the design of their local action Plan.

Our objective is to move ownership of the change plan to local teams.

This is a participative rather than a permissive process.

We expect everyone to participate but no one is licensed to prevent progress. When delegates have issues we design the solutions together.

Teams will self organise and be given ; appropriate support, leadership and when needed go-do-it-direction. This to ensure that everyone delivers their 30-60-90 day plans.

If a team hits amber on two consecutive reviews we send in a dolphin, to help analyse what is working well and what isn't.

Then we resource and Support to deliver the Plan on the next review - if we hit big rocks we call up the Exec and they help us unblock progress.

And we don't rule out having Flipper attach a timed limpet mine to the rear end of any *KIPPERS* who want to block progress. But most of all, we expect to enjoy progress to everyone's real benefit.

We will of course avoid the - early wins quick sand - we've seen that before, fanfares, trumpets, big launch, who ha, with a celebrate success party when we deliver a quick win.

Change groupies will want to say 'Whoopee, this is working. Well done team! Rah Rah! Just like Stars and Stripes with the performing seal. We'll have none of that, thank you very much'.

We expect every team to make solid progress on their local plans, and we listen to what the guys and gals on the sea bed have to say.

As pride in results grows, then of course we join in and celebrate, soberly, professionally with a keen eye on continuous and ongoing improvements.

Jess describes our Can do Purpose and Process

'Our draft *Purpose* that we improve on through dialogue is *'to make this Firth a really; efficient, rewarding, working and living environment for everyone who enjoys being here,'*

Jess sighed and rocked her head a little before her knowing smile and switched on eyes communicated satisfaction with the flip charted starter for ten.

She wasn't quite sure where the words had come from but they must have been in her thinkbox somewhere. After all, she had listened to everyone until her head hurt. Listening and thinking, really was hard work.

But now that she was programmed to listen she had easily recollected simple words that seemed to have an amplified message, her list was;

Success comes in cans not in cants

Listen to what people say first

Work at understanding the other person's message

Where there is a difference in opinions ask the holders of each opinion to say what the other person is saying on the issue

If you are thinking about what you are going to say next, press the pause button, cos you ain't listening

Dolphins think twice as fast as they can squeak, so it is so easy to let the thinkbox take over, judging the message before it has really been said.

Example - not valuing the Sea horse's story or even considering what he was trying to say.

We value everyone's opinion, by listening intently

One voice symbolises a listening team.

Base our decisions on facts …. and this needs a better mind than a mollusc. Molluscs do take everything in, but they then filter out what they think they don't want, and let the rest go. This really is a mind over matter issue.

Dialogue requires an open mind on everything

Take every idea in, then, see where your think box takes you, *thinking inputs will lead to outputs.*

'Granddad, how do we deal with the can't squad, like the limpets who don't want to move on anything, been here forty years, tide in tide out, haven't moved or done anything different in all that time', asked Jess.

'People, limpets, prawns, will resist even the idea of a change for a range of reasons', said Granddad, 'but the most powerful resistance results from fear.

Limpets will be petrified by the thought of moving because they never move. Our cockles had been in the same bed and followed the same work routines for ever, they don't know or understand anything different.

I once heard someone describe resistance as either capability as in - not capable of making the change, versus, just say no - where the no change attitude dominates.

Now whilst the limpets really want to keep on doing what they are doing, when we explained that the dredger was coming, and told them what had happened to the cockles that hadn't moved, they shifted faster than an eel up a sewer pipe.

When we meet group resistance we recognise that we need to give the majority a reason to say yes, we need to listen to what they have to say and design Yes-able propositions.

We'll need compelling reasons for a change, and sometimes the refusniks will need to understand that we have no acceptable alternatives to offer. And that we are happy to consider any that they might have.

With the American invasion force tucked up in Turkey the Bushman could have said to Saddam, 'We are coming to get you, unless you allow free entry and genuinely support our Inspectors'.

And I know they had already said this a number of times, but the sound of the troop carriers landing, and a few more fighters enforcing the no fly zone would have focussed his mind and persuaded him that an environmental change was coming.

If you haven't done everything possible to reach an agreed way forward, how will you sleep if your decisions mean that you will inevitably bomb the country's children?

Now in designing our change process the only thing we want hanging from a rope, is the soap.

We agree the way that we will deal with resistance to change before we start. And we recognise that change automatically creates a tension for everyone with a history especially one where change didn't go well.

Agreeing a process that we use to unblock resistance will be key and we centre this on what is important to all of us. What are our values and what do we stand for?

We canvas opinion through dialogue on our team's values and specifically what everyone can expect if they don't want to change.

Then everyone can make an informed personal choice based on facts.

Change, Survival and Futuring plans need openness and trust

These were the words that Flipper said first when he opened the dialogue session in the river pool, he continued; ' You all know me and I know you, we have come a long way together, been through many a storm side by side.

That said the changes that we need to consider now are bigger than all of us, and ones that requires us to unite behind a powerful plan'.

Flipper was at his passionate best, slightly fearful of presenting, but proud, everyone listened as he continued. 'Today I propose that we draw a line in the sand behind us and that we leave all of our previous differences on the other side of the line.

I have invited one of the very best masters of dialogue this side of Ireland, Jimwatt the kilted Cray fish to guide us through the next few days, but with one precondition.

Every one of us agrees that we will *respect* every single opinion offered with *openness*, and *work at understanding the issues* and ideas - and that we start work right now on building trust in each other.

We give trust first and then we expect to be trusted by others.

Offer your opinions in the knowledge that you will be listened to.

Our Purpose is - 'to make this Firth a really; efficient and rewarding work place and living environment, for everyone who enjoys being here'.

Flipper sat down to great applause.

He hadn't said very much but low air time does breed high trust, and perhaps he was applauded more for his credibility and dependability. Everyone thought that they could build a better future with Flipper as their leader.

Jimwatt went down a storm he had obviously done this before. He gave everyone air time, sifted out the right ideas and threatened to hit Marvin with a mallet if he didn't stop giving Michael a hard time.

His kilt drifted in the current as he walked around each work group growling; *respect everyone's opinion - you give trust then you expect it- success comes in cans - listen to understand.*

The Exec listened to what people said first, in the round table sessions and more importantly at the lunch table and other informal get togethers.

Every wayward input was refocused as needed on our *Purpose - 'to make this Firth a really; efficient, rewarding, working and living environment for everyone who enjoys being here'.*

We did spend a little too much time going down a few sand worm holes, to no great benefit other than the person who took us there knew that they were being valued and listened to.

The Exec met routinely to exchange views on progress and to direction find for the subsequent sessions. Jimwatt updated everyone as ideas progressed into plans. At the end of two days everyone knew that this Plan would succeed.

Grumpus said, 'This is the easy part, thirty delegates in one pool, agreeing a plan, is like falling off a floating log. Easily done, getting the message down to the sea bed and realising everyone's commitment to act is the real challenge'

Jimwatt jumped in with the joker - the card that won the money - when he said 'We need to start off with the big A … we need everyone on this sea bed wanting to make a difference… we need an **Attitude shift'** and here the story turned full circle as they often do.

Jimwatt continued , 'After the Piper Alpha fire, all of the Oil Companies in the North Sea took a good hard look at their Safe Systems of Work, their Risk Assessments, their skills and capabilities and then redesigned their Safe Work Procedures and Systems.

Three years on, and following a big and really expensive initiative, Shell's appraisal of progress left them dissatisfied with the results. They concluded that the planned improvements on *In Control and capable Processes* were inadequate. Following further analysis they concluded that they needed *In Control and capable People* - before the Process tools and techniques would deliver the results.

In more recent times Jimwatt had realised that when Leaders at all levels in an organisation gave a commitment to learning and change. Then displayed the right behaviours in engaging with the people that worked with them - one major blockage to progress - the them-and-us factor, disappeared.

Attitude shift can become the engine of sustained change.
You create the world that you describe and then live in it.

'How will you, the Executive team, the people that everyone looks up to - and appraises - for evidence of change - deliver an Attitude shift?' Jimwatt had stunned the Exec with his question.

A prolonged silence followed until Grumpus broke cover by saying, 'I don't think we can, there is a growing belief that you can't download values and culture and the very spirit of an organisation'.

'We will not be able to describe a change agenda for anyone other than ourselves.

What we can do is create a learning environment that empowers the people who work with us to build a change momentum'.We create our own personal world at work, at home, and for life, through the script that we work to'.

Let me give you an example', said Granddad.

'In reflective moments when I ask myself, why have you worked so hard? I hear a voice in my head that says, 'Right my boy, always do your best'.

It's my Granddad's voice and I listen to a one hundred year old message, given that his experience was fifty years old when he handed it down to me.

Give me a shovel and a pick and a challenge and I am one happy bunny, it's easy to do your best when you just have to drive your own shovel.

With a family history of farming and mining I think I was born to graft and I was joined by a thousand like minded others when we started the Smelter on the side of the Firth, where the cruise ships now dock.

Having started up the smelter, George the Bear, as he was called - on account of his friendly management style - and I, had talked about what we had achieved.

George said 'our people were so pumped up, that if the challenge had been to start up the smelter and then float it out into the Firth, we could have done it.

Our people and teams motivated themselves.

And throughout my life I have found countless numbers of women and men who share my script.

They are proud of who they are and what they do in life and at work.

Most of them can describe times in their work or social lives when they belonged to a high performance team.

And their parents most certainly handed down messages, scripts and genes from a world conquering, self organising, and high performance environment.

These philosophies and work ethics were born out of a common and very often challenging experience that distilled through time into simple messages and behaviours. This is what we need to capture now.

We need to learn new ways of staying competitive, and implement these ideas together'.

'Common Experience, Common Understanding, Common Purpose', said Grumpus, and as they listened to his words the team had another light bulb moment. No one spoke, they just savoured the thoughts.

'How do we help everyone understand the need to grow and change, given that most of us have messages in our heads from the guys who brought us up, and from those who work along side us. What other ponds do we need to swim in to learn and develop a greater understanding of ourselves and others?' Asked Flipper.

'Fish' said Dorcas, everyone gave her that - what are you on look - 'the book about Attitude shift' she said, 'when Grumpus came back from the University I borrowed his notes and a study book called Fish.

If we ask groups to read books together and as a team describe what they think we need to do to deliver - 'Our sea world in 2012' - we can build Common Experience teams and we learn from their new understandings, as well.'

A series of study books were issued to small teams with review sessions leading to mini presentations. Then the chatter started and the learning bug spread quicker than a virus in a fish farm.

We did however run into the long standing problem - word of mouth messaging, you might have heard of it "...send reinforcements we are are going to advance". The story says that it ended up as ..." if you smoke cod liver oil pills you'll end up in a trance".

Somehow Calum, who had a Saturday job as the Calley Thistle Football clubs team mascot ended up reading - The Goal. The grapevine message that he had heard said - as long as you are learning, read anything you like, then advance but no trance.

What a surprise - he had when he read The Goal book - and the Exec had when they reviewed his study presentation. His team of four made a brilliant summary of their ideas from the study and in effect told us how we mobilise everyone towards a competitive and more secure future.

'It's a kind of magic', sang Quentin - the only gay cod fish in Cromarty - when he saw Calum and his team cleaning up the sea bed. They mobilised everyone, the worms digested all the edible waste, the crabs cut up all the large chunks and the flat fish dysoned the whole sea floor.

Everything was recycled, plastic bottles, seaweed cuttings, wet cardboard, paper, collected and compacted in a whale's mouth. Everything had a place and the whole community worked to the new systems.

This proved to be the most powerful message of all. Here was the hard evidence of change and not a word had been spoken. Calum and his team started doing the right things for their work area and when everyone experienced the change they too started to describe something different.

The Clean up team won an Environment Initiative award and the people of Cromarty joined in to celebrate - having the cleanest bottom in the Highlands and Islands!!

Other study book teams provided ideas Leadership on; problem solving, decision making, safe systems of work, performance tools and techniques, and the quality tools of a work environment.

Every team described their own 'Attitude charter', and nominated one Appraiser for all team activities - meetings to ensure that when they did drift away from what they had agreed, the Appraiser called a time out - and they fixed it.

Here was the working example that helped us describe success, *through studying and chatter and doing things, the team had created a Common Experience, through behaviour and practise they created a Common Understanding and from these foundations they created a Common Purpose.*

These changes were team led and aligned well with the Exec's draft plans; fact is they were better than the Exec plan.

The University of Atlantis sent in a team from the Haddock Resources Department. They had a bit of a shock.

'Does this mean that we don't need to carry out attitude surveys to decide if our Colleagues are aligned with the corporate plan'.

'Is anyone really suggesting that you swim in to a work area, ask the guys on the job to explain their Safe Work Process and they can describe it' said another.

'Colin the corporate expert on people and change said 'I don't like this at all', Ingrid interrupted him and said ' I could be out of a job here.'

Quick as a flash Colin the expert on change said, 'Oh no my dear that is not the reason that I don't like the idea, no, er um no'.

Colin didn't convince anyone - his behaviour had already communicated much more than his words.

Everyone around him had **listened to what he had said first – no, er, um –** had failed to communicate conviction. And whilst more words came forth the overall message was different.

There were too many hesitant ah umms and body signals that said, I am worried - this takes me out of my comfort zone - I feel threatened by this.

'We need a plan to cope with this' said Jess, 'an Uh Oh moment plan'.

'What is an Uh – Oh moment', asked Dorcas.

'It's when your body sends you a signal to say that it isn't happy', said Grumpus.

'The bigger the surprise the bigger the Uh-Oh moment', said Granddad.

'In the middle of the IRA bombing campaign in London the organisers of the Bath versus Wigan rugby match at Twickenham decided to announce the match start with a surprise big - bang fire cracker.

Bang!! And for many, their next move was to get up off the floor!

When surprised our body automatically prepares us for what might come next. If the bang really was a bomb then being under the seat was a good place to be!

Driving test jitters, pre-exam nerves, presenters panic or addressing a meeting for the first time, can often trigger Uh-Oh.

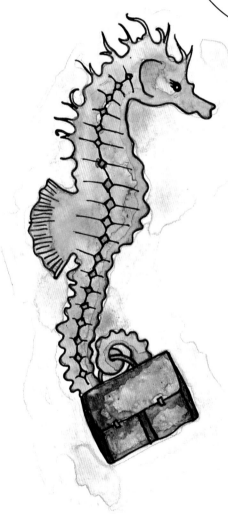

In a change scenario everyone meets Uh Oh

'I think we need a Richter scale to measure comfort zone quakes,' said Grumpus.' We know what happens when we start to feel threatened - Marcia mincing Marvin was now a well worn story - and as we convert ideas into action plans everyone will need to work differently'.

We already know that Calum's team had a stand up with the Clams who refused to clean out the cockle shell closet. When they did wee Quentin was inside, but in the end he was so pleased to be coming out.

The team made him their Appraiser, he didn't half lay down the law. Some said he was a right bitch, and when they did he had a grin like a Culbokie cat, meaaaww just following the rules that we all agreed, purrrrr.

But everyone accepted him for what he was, a really good Appraiser making a valuable contribution to the team.

Quentin's study book had been 'Getting to Yes' and when he had been hiding in the closet he had listened to Calum's team and the Clams collective grievance on why one said they should and the other said they shouldn't.

'Why don't we ask Quentin to form a team to decide how we deal with differences of opinion', said Flipper, and so they did, and that worked to.

The solution was simple - the two Haddock who had been crabbing at each other for weeks over the positioning of the smokies shed, wrote down and signed off what they had been saying on the issue.

A haddock and then B haddock had to repeat what the other had said on the issue. B had repeated A's concerns and A then restated what B had said.

Quentin burst into a songy hum again - 'It's a kind of magic, de dum de dum' and he ran out of words but it didn't matter because the Yes! Yes!! feeling that he felt when Haddie A shook hands with Haddie B - differences settled - through the simple process of understanding what the other party was saying.

Ideas into results gave him a real lift.

This used to take five stages in procedure, at least eight meetings, three appeals, usually stopping just short of a review by Neptune. Who on this occasion was saved from reading a seaweed notes file as thick as a conger eel's belly.

Quentin said 'Jimwatt, this would never have happened before. The Attitude shift is kicking in and gaining momentum, but we do need to listen to both sides of the arguments, change tensions need TLC'.

'TLC - tender loving care!' said Grumpus 'Tender loving care my tail fin and what do you suggest we do when tender loving care doesn't work'.

Try TLC with Dogma the dogfish he'll have a chunk out of your back side before you can say, well stitch my extremities', Grumpus was really worked up and everyone knew it, especially Quentin.

Quentin and Grumpus had had their differences before. Lots of them.

You could say they didn't get on and Quentin who was now armed with the license to grill anyone who wasn't working within the values set, called a timeout right in the middle of Grumpus's rant.

'Grumpus are you being true to our values?' he asked.

'What values, who said anything about TLC applying when you have an angry dog fish biting your aar… tail. Grumpus had paused mid word because he knew the Prawns were listening and that trawler men's language was no longer acceptable.

'Its all right for you sitting there on a rock in the sun, I have to go and present these ideas to my team members. They are going to laugh their little flippers off when I say we have to be nice to a member of the shark family!'

'Well', said Quentin 'if that's you attitude don't bother with any of that line in the sand crap because nothing has changed and nothing will change'.

'Hold on' said Flipper 'I think we can learn a great deal from these exchanges' and just in the nick of time, we all heard bump thud, bump thud.

Dorcas said, 'Let's do something physical, we can work off tension with a good blast at the front of the trawler. Last one there is a human,' she zoomed off through the Sutors and into the Firth.
As they passed Chanonry point they texted Jess and asked for a conference call with Granddad in one hours time. 'Will co - over and out' - Jess sent a text reply.

The whole Pod chattered as they chased the trawler.

'Our Exec need to get their act together' said steady Eddie, 'Can't say one thing and do another when the pressures on' said Jane. Grumpus was on message too, even though he was wide eyed and breathless with the effort of staying ahead of the boat. His think box was however still working away deciding what was best and what next.

Was it Ghandi who said, 'you have to become the change you want to see', he pondered, hmm a bit too complicated perhaps but what about **Change starts with Me**, the tape recorder in his head programmed the message.

Dorcas, Flipper, Grumpus and Tammy dropped off the Pod as they returned from the work out and met up with Jess and Granddad.

Everyone was perturbed about problems and short comings and Jess wrong flippered them all when she said, 'OK let's do dialogue and we'll start off with an input from everyone - on what's working really well'.

Flipper smiled and thought, she's done it again. She's moved us out of *Isn't it awful* and this is wrong and that's wrong and he said bad things and woe is us. We will deal with concern issues later.

Grumpus's contribution was classic ' I have learned so much today by analysing what didn't work that I'm having a breakthrough day'.

When the whole team moved to lessons learned and what do we do differently, Grumpus said, 'when I meet Uh Oh, I am going to pause, take a few deep breaths, relax my body and look up for inspiration.

Quentin showed me the way today and I will always work at understanding the other persons perspective. *I have to be the change I want to see and it starts with me'.*

Change starts with me became one of the Executive team's guidelines.

And out of Grumpus's recent discomfort popped another gem, **'I need to learn how to follow'**, he said. 'Quentin was right when he said that we need to care about other people's opinions, especially when there is a change tension in the air.

I already knew that followership worked in practice from our Pod's fishing system but I now think that this may be the most important factor in leading within an organisation.

Knowing when to lead and when to follow.

Leadership balanced with Followership is also the key to realising the potential of everyone in a team.'

Change starts with me was also adopted as a guideline by all of the delegates at the river pool, and ***Trust, respect, loyalty, listening, basing decisions on facts, leadership, follower-ship and delivering what we promise***.

These were the values that every delegate agreed to work to.

Values to be improved by the work teams and then voted on.

Each work team would nominate a Leader, an Appraiser and a Resource person - sign off their teams own work rules for delivering their 30-60-90 day plan. Resource to organise perform-ance data collection by the team.

Directosaurus, Stewardorex enter a new era

Right ideas x right time x powerful voice x attitude shift = <u>success</u>

When the Lampreys picked up the stones as part of Calum's team clean up they wrote this equation in white stones on the yellow sand. The message could be read through the clear water, helicopter pilots read it and soon the Rosshire journal had pictures of the message on the front page. Change chatter started above the water and travelled far and wide.

The word on the grapevine was that the Madjedski Stadium in Reading was to be the venue for the Easter- difference of opinion - head butt contest.

Directosaurus and Stewardorex were already there with their respective lead teams, pumping it up. And the whole community in the far North realised that to sustain the change they needed; ***the power, commitment to the process, and the resources that only these big guys could deliver.***

The cockles were asked to think about how we communicated the message to the big guys.

They always lazed on their sand bank when the tide ebbed and they just couldn't figure out how they could get a message to these very important people.

Rosemarkie to Reading seemed like mission impossible for a cockle. Then something drew their attention, white stuff dropped from the sky.

'You missed you shiteock' said Sharon as she stretched into the sand and took out her umbrella, 'they'll be back, bomb bays open'

Almost everyone laughed, but the attitude Appraiser cautioned and continued 'I know it's difficult when we're being anointed from a great height. They had agreed to do it over the sea, but there is a bug going around, so perhaps it was a mistake. I will talk to the Seagull team's Appraiser.'

Samantha the seal pup shivered at the water's edge after her first ever dip in the sea. It was 'fffreezing ssshe sssaid' as her white lips chuntered, but her wee thinkbox was working well, 'sssend a ssseagull' she said, answering the cockles quandary.

Her mother almost dropped the welcoming towel when she realised what Mummy's little darling had said. 'I am so proud of her, she is really intelligent you know, takes after my side of the family, I can see my mother in her now, just look at her blond hair and blue eyes'.

Fortunately the Cockles were a listening team and Sharon had picked up the message, 'did you hear that?' Wee Samantha said 'send a seagull'.

What a great idea, they have the capability and the skills set, and come to think of it Seagulls are world class at drawing people's attention.

With a strong tail wind Sammy the seagull arrived at Reading with just three hours flying time and almost needed more time to fully understand how he could deliver the messages.

It was a mind set issue really. There was nothing new in dropping smelly stuff from a great height on to the operating teams below. What he couldn't figure out was how he could drop white stuff on a group called the higher management.

He spent a full forty minutes flying upside down over the stadium trying to work out how he could achieve the feat, then eureka! He looked down and saw both teams warming up at opposite sides of the stadium. Then the penny dropped, when he realised that these higher management guys were exactly the same as the rest of us.

Two sweeps at either end of the stadium and he had everyone's attention - the message stuck even to the keep warm blankets. Sammy addressed both teams separately but with the same message.

He said that 'there was a real passion for change with the teams in the far North, the whole community wanted to work to create a secure future through competitive work - and they need your help'.

Then he hit them with the big one - 'I call on you, the Directosaurus team - renowned for being a group of Managers with an old skills set. And on you -the Stewardorex team - only capable of regurgitating old agreements as a recipe for doing nothing - to adopt our message of *Change starts with me*.'

Their stunned silence gave him strength and the extended pause became a vacuum that he just had to fill, so he continued.

'John Reid thought he had troubles in the Home Office, well some say - you aren't fit for Purpose either.

When did you take time out to learn, study, connect with your Colleagues, and add real value as opposed to trying to do everyone else's day job?

Are you are all working in the same – as, work rituals, rut, where nothing much changes? And given that your wages in both Management and Union are paid for by the chattering classes - hands on people who work hard to add the value that you enjoy I ask you to be mindful.

These guys and gals think a bonus is a bar of chocolate, and that they earn yours for you, and the very least they expect is that you have the same perspective on the facts. They don't want to hear, them and us stories any more'.

He continued, 'now my learned friends, leaders of dolphins and men, I know that the message that I have given you will not be well received.

And I am slightly fearful in relating this to you, because when the Brahan Seer was burned, head down in a barrel of tar, the tar had feathers in it, and I think part of that message was delivered by a seagull!'

Well, talk about shoot the messenger, they might have if they weren't in such deep shock.

More than a penny had dropped that day because both of these teams genuinely thought they were doing a great job.

'Fact is that when you don't explore other people's perspectives, *Groupthink* follows. Read up on Irving Janis' he screeched ' consider his analysis of US decision making.

Ask yourselves, are your organisations handicapped by powerful voices over riding alternative opinions?

'And what will happen when someone gets around to analysing Iraq? We'll find the same isolation of people who dissent from the powerful party lines.

What will we remember Robin Cook for, God bless him', said the seagull 'he flies with us now.

And we think you need to progress your business and members interests with at the very least a common understanding on the facts.

Then you can add your power to your working Communities Purpose - this to include competitive security.

Now Sammy was a Scottish seagull ye ken and he wondered if his message had diluted through translation frae Buckie to Berkshire because no one said a word.

There was a prolonged silence and then someone started to clap, slowly, methodically, persistently, and others joined in. Then the Union team started to walk towards the centre of the stadium to a rhythmic, drum like beat.

Then the Management team did the same thing.

Sammy had heard this sound before when Scotland scored at Murrayfield and he thought be-jings, I am going to witness the biggest Gang bang heed butt session since Culloden.

Let's take a time out, he screamed, 'Time out', and then he squawked the ultimate threat – 'If you don't stop - I will - I'll fly over your heads with the bomb bay doors open', But he needn't have worried.

Both teams came together in the centre of the stadium, shook hands and agreed to meet in the Highlands for a review.

British Airways sponsored the flights. They already knew what was going to happen in a pre holiday period, the baggage handlers were going to beat up the bosses with the *BATNA* .

What an advert for the travelling world, thank goodness for the French or otherwise we'd be top of this European league.

These pages are for your notes

Change was in the air

'Doors to manual' said the pilot as the plane flew right over the Cromarty Firth and circled to engage the Westerly wind on its tail. As soon as the big guys left the plane they noticed a very obvious change, this was a different world and at least one pullover colder than the south. They quickly acquainted with the Moray Firth on the Kessock Bridge, and the Cromarty firth on the Foulis Ferry Bridge.

Brahan Seer the futurist, came to mind first as the Cromarty Firth had a gaggle of one eyed monsters at anchor. Oil rigs were parked up and serviced in its sheltered waters, the newer rigs have six legs - but to this day they still present a long neck- one eyed monster image.

And then on to the Salvesen House, owned by the Munro Clan since 1660, housed their family until 1923 when the Salvesen family - of shipping fame -moved in.

Twelve bedrooms, sixteen acres, a snip at just over £1million said the recent advert in the Times, but needs TLC and clever landscaping.

They forgot to mention the Alness River and the salmon pool, where everyone was already gathered.

The Director of all things Waterful - the most senior Management person with an influence on work and life in the Firth.

And the National President of the brothers, sisters and United Fisher folk.com - the Director's equivalent in the Union - were given the front seats.

Jolly Jane stood erect at her flip chart, proud to have been chosen, her voice carried clearly from one side of the river to the other, when she said, 'Thank you for coming to meet with us. We represent a living community with a great heritage.

Our environment is changing, as the world around us changes, and we believe that we need to address our local change agenda ahead of the time', she paused and everyone clapped.

Then even more inspired, she took a deep deliberate breath and continued, 'This is our Purpose', turning the page on the flip chart, it read;

"To make this Firth a really; efficient, rewarding, working and living environment for everyone who enjoys being here."

'I will coordinate this conference', said Jane 'and introduce presentations from my Colleagues - but first I need to communicate what we think is important to us in delivering our Plans.

From our dialogue to date, we know that we need to deliver, we need to win, but the manner of winning is important to us.

These are the words that represent what every one of us is prepared to give - to each other and to you our guests and visitors;

Trust, respect, loyalty, listening, we also value decisions based on facts, leaders who know when to follow, and a commitment to delivering what we promise.

Teams presented their study books, and at the end of each presentation tribal pride kicked in as the delegates from each team's sea-bus applauded and cheered. Many of them were hearing their own ideas now adopted as team speak.

Calum wore his Caledonian Thistle shirt and another team member his Ross Sutherland rugby jersey. Their presentation on

'The Goal' was superb they challenged everyone in the audience with questions and even showed a video of Lean flow production on the Lamprey stone moving project.

They summarised and closed with the principles of Lean workflows and In Control and Capable Work Processes - and handed on seamlessly to Dorcas who let her team do all the talking as they presented - 'Our road map to In Control and Capable People.'

The Director and the President were engulfed in a high tide of enthusiasm and when wee Quentin presented 'Getting to Yes', he just flaunted all the way through, and to music, he had the other Queen singing on a tape.

'It's a kind of Magic', everyone joined in with background flipper clapping and tail swinging ... It's a kind of magic, it's a kind of magic, one dream, one goal, one soul, one prize, one golden glance of what should be……. one shaft of light that shows the way….. this flame that burns inside of me … I'm here in secret harmony...

The whole place was rocking and because it was our Quentin and the songs words connected with our issues, it was like having our very own tribute band concert. [Listen to the words in the Queen music here].

Everyone stood, the applause went on for an age, and Quentin wasn't sure what to do next because he hadn't given his key words messages as yet.

He just milked the applause, curtseyed with one flipper finger under his chin as he stooped. Then he raised both flippers into the air into- be silent position- and the crowd hushed.

'Since we started our Visioning and Actions process, we realised that Freddy Mercury might well be related to the Brahan Seer.

He was undoubtedly another visionary, and when he sang ; one goal, one prize, one dream, one destiny, these words describe our circumstance and agenda here today.

We have drawn a line in the sand and through our action plans and working together we really do have a powerful but secret harmony.'

He then approached the big guy's chairs and said, 'after lunch you will visit the teams on the sea floor and be able to review ideas in action.

As you do, please remember that we need you to become - and he broke into song, 'the shaft of light that shows the way', because we all recognise that we really do have, 'only one golden glance of what should be'.

This Firth has had a thousand years of local magic, but we need you to be describing something similar to our ideas – to enable us to move towards a secure future based on open harmony'.

'It's a kind of magic, there can be only one, one goal, one dream, one destiny' played out again as he walked back to his team to prolonged applause from everyone. They all communicated through silent pumped up pride, ready to flow eyes, and smiles like water melons.

Granddad filled up, so Jess did too, and Grumpus organised a group huddle with Tammy, Dorcas, Jimwatt, Flipper and Quentin who by this time was now blubbering over everyone.

So much work and effort had come together around a few simple messages, superbly delivered by people who cared.

After lunch we jumped on to a fleet of small boats at the jetty. The big guys visited the work projects, saw the data collection and the recording of where we were against each plan.

All of the performance data was recorded and communicated by working members of the teams. ***Our plans, our work areas, our numbers, our future***, this was really impressive but most of all on every single project - ***Colleague behaviour - and the way the work places looked - communicated pride from all.***

Pride in themselves, in their performance and this really did have a magic of its own.

And the Director and the President felt fulfilled too, they found that they had more in common with each other than they thought.

They had been angry with the Seagull at the stadium.

How dare he dive in and say what he had said, but he was right.

They were spending too much time trying to do everyone else's job, and getting sucked down into the day to day.

They asked Granddad and Jimwatt to distil the formulae and recipe of the Cromarty Firth teams as they intended to introduce similar principles in their own teams, back at base.

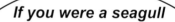

Summarising as the sun sets

There is no better place in the world to distil things than the Highlands of Scotland. And as the Exec watched the sun go down over the peaks of Wester Ross, two things came into a brilliant silhouetted outline - the mountains in the west - and in their minds and equally impressive, their memories of what the individuals and teams had delivered today.

'This is awesome' said Grumpus, 'I didn't realise what talent we had in our teams, and yes Quentin did steal the show with the story he told through the music, what a show stopper, but everyone delivered'.

'Can't say I'm surprised', said Granddad,' In my experience it's always the same. Organisations don't even start to understand the power and potential that exists within the people who work along side them'.

'Well', said Jess using a phrase she had heard from the Director, 'let's pump through to the bottom line, what are the three to five most important factors in achieving what we have to date?'

Everyone's list was summarised as follows -

The Exec describe an outline for future success and security, under a simple unifying Purpose, with perhaps a few ideas on how we get there

Exec describe team basics and specifically the way to manage differences

Then keep it as simple as you can, do something that aligns with the Purpose

Connect with the teams on the sea floor, on their work agenda through local actions, visible plans, teams collect data, support when needed

And in tandem with everyone doing something, mobilise team talent, allow talented individuals and teams to show the way forward

Resource the plan. Some talent will need to level down, but before you start ensure that the talent is equal to or is greater than the challenge

Take the majority with you and work hard with those who resist changes.

Look after the minority who won't be happy working in the new way, and help them work somewhere else

Change starts with me and for those that can't- In love there is justice – you do need to move on.

Will the President and the Director be happy?

'We haven't really given them much to work on,' said Dorcas.

Grumpus said, 'I think that our Colleagues gave them the answers that they need. Fact is you just cannot download values, culture or a team working vision.

I think they understand that their role is to build a storm jetty around their change agents and support competitive work systems and structures. And most of all empower the people who work for them to create the Attitude shift.'

'They need to sponsor Purpose aligned examples of what works'

'If we are right in this summary, then it would be wrong for us to try and describe the answer for their organisations. The players in their teams need to describe it to them, the way our teams did today.'

Corporation Leaders authorise million pound spends to download stuff that just disappears into the sand.

Videos, glossies, monthly this and that's. With endless journeys, to timeless meetings, achieving diddly squat.

Month after month becomes year after year, and who in their own organisation is going to tell them?

'Sounds like a barrel of tar job to me', said Tammy.

They will have to describe it for themselves.

The Union Presidents men need to get off the political treadmill and be sure that they still have a job. There are too many snipers in the undergrowth at present for them to address the real change agenda.

Directors are fired if they don't deliver the numbers, and get big fat cheques if they do. Simple choice really. You feed the bear that writes the bonus cheques, it's the reward system that's wrong.'

These leaders of men work in a tough environment and it takes real bravery to stand out against the *Groupthink*. You almost need to have had the big bonuses so that you become rich enough to take the risk.

And whilst there is always a lot of noise from the anti fat cat choir, there are very few who could change places and do the job effectively.

It would be really useful if the Presidents men and the Director could describe the same version of the facts. Then they could spread the gospel all the way to the White House. Ideally before we invade Iran.

Time for bed.

What a great day.

Today the Cromarty Firth.

And tomorrow well who knows?...

I have one more question

'Why did Pliny's Grumpus have to go?' Asked Jess.

'From what I have seen and heard all of the Grumpus family have been a fantastic source of history and knowledge throughout the ages'.

'Well Jess,' said Granddad, 'it's all about timing.

There is a time to arrive, and you have timed this perfectly, your time is now. You are intelligent, quick, inquisitive, caring, great to be around, and you aren't blocked by too much history.'

'There is also a time to leave, and hopefully I'll get the chance to say goodbye to everyone, before I leave.

Now, the dolphins have this down to a fine art. They are very self aware, and you will see the older flippers drift off on their own for an hour - then a week - then a month. So the Pod, and especially the youngsters get used to them not being there.'

'And while they are away something magical happens, the Pod thinks about them more than when they were there. The guidance messages like - *only chatter by saying things that you can be proud of* - become more meaningful and important.

Pups remember the things they did with Grumpus, and the places they went, and what happened when they had this or that problem.

Right the way through to one or two really happy memories where they connected at a higher level and surfed the waves together'

'Then of course the oldies come back into the Pod', said Granddad, 'and there are more good memories to call on. Over a few years of absences they build up such a store that they reach the - tipping point -where the Pod has so many memories and stories that give everyone a lift through the telling.

From this point on, when the oldies really are away they are actually ever present, always connecting, through memory or message or song or image or smell or sound or flower. All of our senses were designed to connect us with the contents of our memory banks'.

Everyone was silent, Grumpus started to de de de dede de dum dum, as the breeze lifted and the tide came closer. He had a great singing voice.

Buster took out his violin and caught Grumpus's melody with a soulful calm introduction.

Grumpus joined in on exactly the right beat and sang, 'when I am down and all my soul so weary, when troubles come and my heart burdened be, then I am still and wait here in the silence, until you come, and sit a while with me. You raise me up, so I can stand on mountains, you raise me up to walk on stormy seas, I am strong when I am on your shoulders, you raise me up to more than I can be'.

'Play this tune and message at our funerals', said Grumpus, Granddad nodded, 'then smile and remember that we are still smiling with you', said Grumpus.

'This world was a great place to be in our time, but now it's your time, and we want you to remember us with a smile.

Think about us often.

Swim with us. Breathe us in with long deep breaths. Look up to the blue or cloudy or star lit sky and smile. Together we'll help raise you up to more than you can be - for ever and ever.'

And this should be our call to the big guys with power. Leave this life having added value to those who walked it with you.

Download a heritage in memories and messages that the chattering classes will be proud to retell.

It will be the truths of life that turn out to be important, and the same applies to the life of an Organisation.

Time spent at work can become a waste when the organisation's people play Games - build small minded fantasy worlds. Where the facts can't be seen through the darkness.

Apply the grapevine test to every message -
is this fact or is it fiction.

Leaders - you are the people who have the power to create an environment where everyone can speak their minds and know that they will be listened to.

Where there are political logics and groups of people describing the same circumstances differently, demand an open dialogue.

It's only the game players who won't want open exchanges.

Games need to be covert, under cover activities usually scripted to retain personal power.

Games must stop

Give the people that walk this world with you the freedom of a choice, based on facts.

And remember that our history to date catalogues progress made through tough challenges.

Complacency will not deliver break through change.

Describe a competitive future and in that expect your Colleagues Attitude to be the best. *Settle for nothing less.*

Secure Organisations need - a Common Purpose and their Teams - something to work towards.

One golden glance of what should be.

Every one of us can become that shaft of light that shows the way.

When Change starts with me behaving differently.

As you read this page you are very close to the end of our story. If the read has helped you connect with ideas for your organisation then our ending is your beginning.

Start your journey towards a competitive future by forming a small Executive team to describe your organisation five years from now.

Include your understanding of best practise and test this with other organisations and experts in work related fields.

How many European organisations are at the top of the wave, scrambling to stay afloat, with their Executives sucked down into day to day working detail. Their leaders are experts at managing the crisis and overcoming problems that shouldn't have happened in the first place.

We listened to one organisation's voice, where the workforce gave a clear message to their Leaders, on securing a competitive future. *Give us a plan that we can deliver on*. The leaders did just that and the performance turnaround was superb.

When your work Colleagues are able to describe their role in a competitive future, you are a Leader.

Write your story, press the change starts with me button and help create a better future for everyone.

Revisit your post it notes - you have already started to write your organisations story.

Internet References

Pliny the Elder search on this name - Quotations page is useful

Pliny the Younger- search on this name

Dolphins- search on this name - Wikopedia connects with Pliny

Brahan Seer search this name or follow Clan Mackenzie

The Black Isle - Scotland search on this name

www.ericberne.com leads to Games People Play

Amazon.co.uk search on Thought bubbles and think boxing

Amazon.co.uk search on The Tipping point

Amazon.co.uk search on The Goal

Amazon.co.uk search on Group Think

Wikopedia search on Group Think is worth a review

It's a kind of Magic – Queen is available for purchase on internet download

You lift me up - Josh Groban version is available for purchase on internet download

Thoughts from Queen

It's a kind of magic, it's a kind of magic, a kind of magic
One dream, one soul, one prize, one goal
One golden glance of what should be
It's a kind of magic
One shaft of light that shows the way
No mortal man can win this day
It's a kind of magic
The bell that rings inside your mind
Is challenging the doors of time
The waiting seems eternity
A day will dawn on sanity
Is this the kind of magic
There can be only one
This reign that lasts a thousand years
Will soon be done
This flame that burns in side of me
I'm here in secret harmony
The bell that rings inside your mind
Is challenging the doors of time
This is the kind of magic
This reign that lasts a thousand years will soon be done
It's a kind of magic

Thoughts from Jimwatt to the same music

The reign that lasts a thousand years
They never ever come
We mortals have a shorter span
And make a chance from one
There is a kind of magic
When workmates see the light
That shines within each one of them
Just waiting to ignite
We need that secret harmony
That's built on trust and care
When we describe a future that everyone can share
The bell must ring inside our minds
Just listen in, its there
This is a kind of magic
There will be more than one
And when we work together the future's just begun

Thoughts from Josh Groban

When I am down and Oh my soul so weary
When trouble comes and my heart burdened be
Then I am still and wait here in the silence
Until you come and sit a while with me

You raise me up so I can stand on mountains
You raise me up to walk on stormy seas
I am strong when I am on your shoulders
You raise me up to more than I can be

You raise me up so I can stand on mountains
You raise me up to walk on stormy seas
I am strong when I am on your shoulders
You raise me up to more than I can be

Thoughts from Dorcas to the same tune

When spirits join the bond is strong and timeless
Look forward with a boldness and with care
And when you need look up and see the star light
Then breathe me in and join us once again

For I am strong when I am on your shoulders
There is a light, a strength for evermore
For we were joined through love and touch and kindness
I'm always there and caring more and more

When spirits join the bond is strong and timeless
Once joined they never, never ever part
And we give strength to those we leave behind us
With every tear new promise has to start

You raise me up so I can stand on mountains
With you I am much more than only me
For I am strong when I am on your shoulders
You raise me up to more than I can be

Games your organisation doesn't want to play

NJ niggle joke from the wind up man
NIGYSOB now I have got you son of a bitch - payback time
IGYAM I'll give you the monkey
IIWIIDHAWL I would love to help But with assorted reasons why
you can't
IItAWFUL this is wrong, that's wrong, guess what management
have done now
WCWBFThis, the blame game [watch the Apprentice on UK TV]
KIKA persecute another individual or tribe
NKOTB new kid on the block-old power brokers behave badly
KIPPERS knowledge is power people expect ransoms
DUFINFO deliberately give wrong information
OMAGS overtime magicians who create work rackets
NoINFO exclude people from information loops
MyGang we are OK but everyone else is a Dodo
BOHICA bend over here it comes again
LHGIam look how good I am-dumbo
AgMags agreement magicians conjuring Cants
SAgMags power brokers who abuse Safety
WOTNOBS we are not talking to you because
CANTsquad eighty four reasons why we can't
Directorsaurus list of out of date leaders
Stewardorex interpreter of ancient agreements
WALDO we always do it this way - usually my way
GATME gospel according to Me
SQUINTS status quo interpreters
KNEWTYS knew what to do yesterday
WHENWES when we worked somewhere else we did it this way
GRAVY Trainers-tickets to ride but not to work
LUMPER promise me a redundancy cheque - then I'll be normal
UMPERLUMPER I'll be normal for a really really big cheque.
MYWAY as sung by Frank Sinatra – I did it my way

And the credits are all yours

In memory of one of the best self organising teams, where Opinion formers and Leaders at all levels in the organisation delivered with pride – Briton Ferry Steel Company 1893 -1978.

With respect to; Foyers, Kinlochleven, Invergordon and Lochaber, all Highlands of Scotland smelters with over one hundred years of high performance team work, from 1895 to 2009.

In recognition of the Farmers and Coal Miners who shift worked the coal and the land in the South Wales valleys, a Community partnership at its very best, where people pulled together and supported each other.

In celebration of the rugby playing communities all over the world, and to the bonds and never ending friendship that the game produces.

And to working communities and organisations where people meet to make things and to help each other develop and grow.

With credit to the Trade Union Leaders who understand the benefits of working together, as opposed to the tribal urge to my-gang , separate and divide.

With equal credit to the Leaders at all levels in organisations who can describe where their work team is going and have developed the skills set to take people with them.

And last but not least to the dolphins –

Rolly Adams, Arthur Kyte, John Petersen, Raymond Thomas,
Bertie Melin, Arthur Bevan, Jack Lewis, Percy Bishop
at Briton Ferry Steel.

Gordon Drummond, George Haggart, Jim Hall, Hugh Clark
GMB, Peter Baxter, Bill Kennedy, Brendan Darcy, Jock Comloquoy,
Billy, Davy, Malcolm, Richard, Sabena, Doreen, Sandy Patience,
Murdo McIver, Allan - Invergordon

Martin Wibberley, Nigel Thomas, Hilary Mills, and Phil Grant
on the Bosch Cardiff start up.

David Underwood, Simon Harris, Ruth Maxwell,
Debra Llewellyn, Val Thoburn and Mairead Wharton
on the Valeo Gorseinon start up.

Viv DuFeu the lawyers lawyer at Eversheds and Capital Law.

Bob Miller, Mike Edwards, Jim Watson on the Sun Valley, Balliol
start up.

Mike Burnand and Stuart Smith
in their turn around time at Lucas-Sumitomo.

Adrian Burleton, Mike Sturt, Nigel Owen, Fiona Bailey
at Safeway UK.

Brian Buckland, Harry and the minus twenty Planners team
at Caradon Catnic

Moira Classe, Head Teacher, St Mary's Bathgate, Primary
School - Falkirk.

Heather Darcy, Head Teacher, Craigentiny Primary School Edinburgh.

Mike Harris and the world class pod at Logan Aluminum - USA

Robert Langmead, Jim, James, Shirl, Steve, Andy and the new pod in California

Laurence Faircloth, Eddie, Mel, Lynda Johnson and Bob Lazmirski - Rogerstone.

Champs, Gary, Sharon, Dave, Roy, Brian, Jimmy, Diane, Dee, Mike Sturt at Sainsburys.

Dave Williams, Penny Haworth, Mike Tyson, Roger Bradley , Barry Trace, Ron Park, Ian McLardie, Alan Morrison, Bill Beaumont, Kev James, Paul Maddock, Vern Edmondson, Dougie Duncan, Nigel Thomas and Brian Ward for helping form a new pod at Eskmeals, Cumbria.

To families everywhere and to Caroline Bevan an Elim Church change leader who went home, with love to us all, April 17th 2007. **You lift us up to more than we can be.**